Decorating Techniques

Joaquim Chavarria

WATSON-GUPTILL PUBLICATIONS/NEW YORK

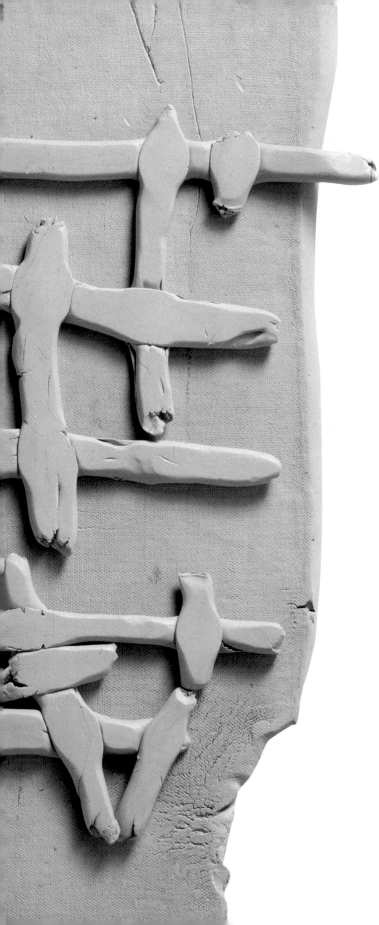

Ceramics Class: Decorating Techniques
Original Spanish title:
    Aula de céramica: Decorácion
Editorial director: María Fernanda Canal
Production director: Rafael Marfil
Text and exercises: Joaquim Chavarria
Graphic Design: Carlos Bonet
Diagrams: SET, Serveis Editorials i Tècnics
Layout: Pacmer, S.A.
Photography: Nos & Soto
Archive research: Mª Carmen Ramos
Translation: Jonathan Bennett

First published in the United States in 2000 by Watson-Guptill
Publications, a division of VNU Buisness Media, INC
770 Broadway, New York, N.Y. 10003-9595
www.watsonguptill.com

Copyright © 1998 Parramón Ediciones, S.A.
Gran Via de les Corts Catalanes, 322-324
08004 Barcelona. Spain

Library of Congress Catalog Card Number: 99-69152
ISBN 0-8230-0594-1

Manufactured in Spain

2 3 4 5 6 / 04 03 02

CONTENTS

INTRODUCTION

It is not difficult to understand how ceramic artists in ancient times first came to decorate their pieces. A material as malleable as clay readily shows the finger marks on its surface that are invariably left during the shaping process. Such marks might have suggested the beginnings of a decoration; imagination did the rest.

As time progressed and as new ceramics processes were discovered, decorative methods increased. Since those early impressions made by chance, other, more deliberate techniques were developed, using lines and shapes that may be angular and geometric, ornate and flowery, or like animals or people. The introduction of metal oxides and colored clays added color.

Enshrined in their ceramics, different cultures have left decorations that have shown us not only the level of perfection they achieved but also their way of life and their customs, in scenes of war, domestic life, religion, and more.

As in any art form, before creating any work, it is vital to study the materials and the general processes. Although it might seem that decoration is something that only affects the surface of a ceramic piece, it should be conceived as an integrated part of the entire piece. The decoration chosen in each case depends on the artist's intentions. Once a piece has reached an aesthetically finished form it can be finished with a simple glaze, or it can be covered with highly complex decorations.

As each work progresses the ceramist must decide which method or methods of decoration will be the most appropriate. Decoration does not necessarily demand complex techniques; often less sophisticated ones work best. The most important factor is to choose a method that fits the overall design of the piece. Study a bit about the different methods of decoration and do some experimenting to learn about the possible results each can yield. With practice you'll be able to determine which method is best suited for each piece, although in the beginning you may find you occasionally need to start the decorating process from the beginning again, or in some cases even start a whole new piece.

All the pieces featured in this book have been chosen for the express purpose of teaching the decorative process, but keep in mind that they show only a part of what can be achieved; use your imagination to discover even more. Most pieces require only a minimum of manual dexterity, though some necessitate practice in drawing and painting. For the more complicated designs, always plan them out on paper first. You may also want to try them out on test pieces before applying to the actual items.

Remember that in the creative process there are no set rules, nor is one system "better" than another, only more appropriate to a particular case. The final result should be a combination of the right choices throughout the process: materials, construction techniques (modeling, throwing, molding), decoration methods, glazing, and firing. Again, this knowledge will come with study and practice.

I hope that the examples shown in this book will serve as the start of a long and productive road that takes students as far as they wish. To all I offer my best wishes.

Joaquim-Manuel Chavarria Climent

METHODS OF DECORATION

When creating work in clay, the method of decoration is almost as important as the way the piece is shaped, molded, or thrown. When conceptualizing a piece, it is important to know which method of decoration will be the most suitable to provide perfect harmony between the different elements of material, shape, size, texture, color, and so on.

Ceramics decoration can be divided into five groups, according to the state of the clay: soft, damp pieces; leather-hard pieces; dry pieces; bisque-fired pieces; and glazed pieces.

Menhir I & III, 1984. 15³/4 x 2³/4 x 2³/4 in. (40 x 7 x 7 cm) and 25³/8 x 4 x 3¹/2 in. (64.5 x 10 x 9 cm). Firing temperature: 2282°F (1250°C).

Decorating soft, damp pieces. In this state the clay can be adorned with imprints, textures, and incisions, as well as by mixing different colors of clay.

1. Stoneware with grog; modeled from solid clay, imprinted, and hollowed out.

2. Stoneware with medium-grained grog; modeled from textured solid clay and hollowed out.

3. Thrown red clay and china clay; agate finish.

4. Egyptian paste.

Vase, 1994. 10 x 5 x 3³/8 in. (25.5 x 13 x 8.5 cm). Firing temperature: 2282°F (1250°C).

Bowl, 1982. 3¹/2 x 4³/4 in. (9 x 12 cm). Firing temperature: 1760°F (960°C).

Boat and Owl, 1998. 5¹/2 x 2³/4 x 2 in. (14 x 7 x 5 cm) and 3 x 2 x 2 in. (7.5 x 5 x 5 cm). Firing temperature: 1760°F (960°C).

Decorating leather-hard pieces. Clay that is semi-rigid can still be manipulated using sgraffito (a scraping method), cutting, carving, encrusting with other clay, and decorating with engobes (resists, marbling, combing, burnishing, and the like).

5. Stoneware; thrown, carved, with engobe.

6. Stoneware with coarse grog; slab-modeled with added reliefs.

7. Red clay; thrown, with engobe and glaze.

Conglomeration, 1976. 15³/8 x 6 x 5¹/2 in. (39 x 15 x 14 cm). Firing temperature: 2300°F (1260°C).

Bowl, 1984. 7⁷/8 x 8⁵/8 in. (20 x 22 cm). Firing temperature: 2300°F (1260°C).

Vase, 1974. 7⁷/8 x 4³/4 in. (20 x 12 cm). Firing temperature: 1760°F (960°C).

Decorating dry pieces. In this state the form can no longer be altered, but it can be painted with oxides and pigments; a surface covered with oxides or engobes can be scraped (sgraffito), and resists can be made with wax, latex, paper, or objects.

8. Stoneware with coarse grog; slab-built, incised, carved, and decorated with oxides.

Decorating bisque-fired pieces. These can be painted in various ways with pigments, metallic oxides, and enamels.

9. Thrown stoneware; underglazed decoration.

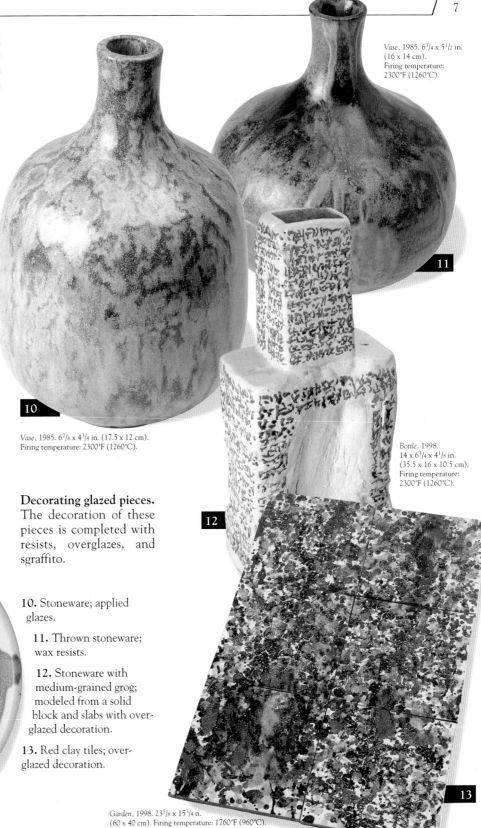

Vase, 1985. 6³/₄ x 5¹/₂ in. (16 x 14 cm). Firing temperature: 2300°F (1260°C).

Sculpture, 1982. 14¹/₂ x 9 x 2 in. (37 x 23 x 5 cm). Firing temperature: 2282°F (1250°C).

Vase, 1985. 6⁷/₈ x 4³/₄ in. (17.5 x 12 cm). Firing temperature: 2300°F (1260°C).

Bottle, 1998. 14 x 6³/₄ x 4¹/₈ n. (35.5 x 16 x 10.5 cm). Firing temperature: 2300°F (1260°C).

Decorating glazed pieces. The decoration of these pieces is completed with resists, overglazes, and sgraffito.

10. Stoneware; applied glazes.

11. Thrown stoneware; wax resists.

12. Stoneware with medium-grained grog; modeled from a solid block and slabs with overglazed decoration.

13. Red clay tiles; overglazed decoration.

Plate, 1982. 7¹/₂ in. diam. (18.5 cm). Firing temperature: 2300°F (1260°C).

Garden, 1998. 23⁵/₈ x 15³/₄ n. (60 x 40 cm). Firing temperature: 1760°F (960°C).

MATERIALS

The materials described below are used both for creating and for decorating ceramic objects. In each exercise I have chosen the clay that I consider the best suited to the method of decoration, although this does not mean that it was the only appropriate choice.

The clays and engobes are colored with oxides and pigments. Together with the glazes, these give ceramics their color.

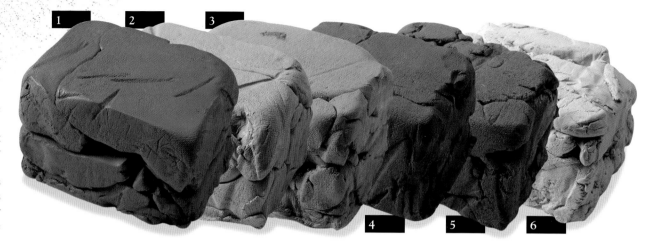

1. Red clays contain iron oxide, from which they get their color. Their elasticity makes them useful both for modeled pieces and for thrown ones. Firing temperature varies from 1742 to 2030°F (950–1110°C).

2. Ball clays are characteristically white or ivory because there is no iron-bearing clay in their composition. These clays are glazed after firing. There are three types of ball clay: soft, mixed, and hard. Firing temperature varies from 1760 to 2372°F (960–1300°C).

3. Stoneware clays, after firing, are impermeable, opaque, and vitrified, and may be white, beige, gray, ivory, or brown in color. Firing temperature varies from 2102 to 2372°F (1150–1300°C).

4–5. Clays containing grog acquire ochre tones after firing. The grog creates texture in the finished piece. Firing temperature varies from 2102 to 2372°F (1150–1300°C).

6. Porcelain clays, after firing, acquire a very pure white color. They may be translucent if they are less than 1/8 inch (3 mm) thick. Firing temperature varies from 2282 to 2372°F (1250–1300°C) for soft clay, and 2486 to 2660°F (1380–1460°C) for hard clay.

7. Metal oxides are among the materials used in the process of decoration. Here, from left to right, are copper, nickel, chrome, cobalt, iron, copper carbonate, cobalt carbonate, iron chromate, lead chromate, and manganese dioxide. These materials are found in very small percentages in the composition of engobes and glazes, and are weighed with high-precision scales.

8. Detail of copper carbonate oxide.

9. Other materials are ceramic pigments used in underglazes and overglazes and also in the preparation of engobes. They are diluted with water and applied onto dry and bisque-fired pieces or onto raw or fired glaze. It is advisable to mix them with 10 percent glaze or transparent glaze.
A. lilac, red, rose, carmine; B. yellow, orange, light yellow, yellowish orange, brown; C. dark green, light green, emerald green, forest green; D. ultramarine blue, light blue, sky blue; E. black

10. Detail of carmine pigment.

TOOLS

Paintbrushes are used for applying engobes, glazes, pigments, and oxides. They are also used for patterning borders and applying underglaze and overglaze decorations. It is helpful to have various shapes and sizes for different types of decoration.

Wooden paddles of different shapes and sizes are used in the modeling process as well as to create textures and make paddled imprints. Some are flat for working on flat surfaces; others are convex for working on concave surfaces.

Rubber bulb blows air (such as for removing dust) or is used to apply liquid materials such as glazes and engobes.

Trimming tools consist of a wooden handle with a wire in one of a variety of shapes, on one or both ends. They are used for hollowing out pieces that are modeled from blocks of clay, and to even up, smooth, and add grooves to surfaces.

Cutters of tin or other materials have a cutting edge that is pushed downward onto the clay to cut small pieces accurately from thin slabs. They can also be used to make openwork.

Knives are usually made of hard wood, although they can also be made of plastic or other materials. They are used in modeling for joining, luting, smoothing, polishing, creating texture, and the like. For more versatility, they have a different shape at each end.

Potter's needles and punches have a metal point set into a wooden handle. They are used to mark, scrape, lute, and create openwork pieces.

Metal modeling tools, knives, and scalpels are used for cutting, incising, creating openwork, and doing sgraffitto.

Canvas, rolling pin, and wooden slats are used in the preparation of ceramics. To keep the clay from sticking to the work surface it is laid on the canvas, between two slats of the same thickness. Using the rolling pin the clay is then rolled flat, until it is the same thickness as the slats.

Metal ribs are used to make pieces on a wheel, to smooth surfaces, and to burnish thrown pieces.

Mortar and pestle may be made of glass or porcelain. They are used to grind and mix ceramic materials, both wet and dry.

DECORATING SOFT, DAMP PIECES
IMPRESSIONS AND TEXTURES

Imprinted designs have been used to decorate pieces since ceramics were first created. After the piece has been shaped, it can be marked with various textures and different motifs using your fingers, various objects and tools, or by making a stamp to create a particular texture.

Because the pieces have to be soft for the impression to be effective, they should be handled with care. Also, with open forms (such as bowls or boxes), it is necessary to support the walls on the inside so that they do not become deformed. With closed forms (bottles, vases, and the like), be sure to use a clay type and a thickness that will keep its shape.

Pieces that are modeled from slabs of clay have the advantage that the designs can be imprinted before the clay is cut out. It is then left until it reaches leather-hardness before it is handled.

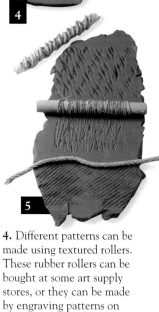

1. Examples of the impressions and textures made with a fingernail and the tip of a finger on a slab of red clay.

2. Examples of a slab of clay printed using the handle of a potter's needle, the end of a square piece of wood, and two small objects.

3. The ends of wooden knives or toothpicks can be used to create different textures.

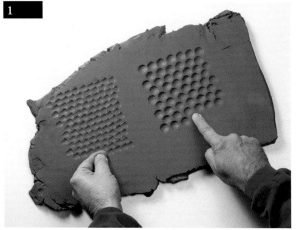

4. Different patterns can be made using textured rollers. These rubber rollers can be bought at some art supply stores, or they can be made by engraving patterns on cylinders made of wood or plaster.

5. Try rolling string across a slab of soft clay, or winding the string around wooden cylinders and then rolling it.

6. Small plaster stamps can make interesting reliefs.

7. A sample of patterns made from different materials: canvas, hessian, and a creased cloth.

8. Organic elements such as rice, nut shells, fruit pits, leaves, bark, and other items can produce a great variety of textures.

TEXTURES

*T*his bottle was made from slabs of stoneware and fine-grained grog. As with all objects made from slabs of clay, care must be taken when preparing and handling the material. Care must also be taken when rolling the small wooden roller over the clay to make the imprint. Before working with the clay, carve a pattern on a wooden roller to create the relief, or use a purchased roller.

Make the impression as soon as you have prepared the slabs of clay, then leave the clay to harden for a few hours before working on it further. If you handle the slabs too soon, the sides of the bottle will lose their shape.

1. With a rolling pin and two 3/8-inch (8 mm) slats, prepare a slab of clay to make a square-based bottle. Use a wooden knife to trace the outlines of four rectangles and two squares.

2. Roll the patterned roller over the surface of the slab to imprint the pattern on the clay.

3. Let the clay harden somewhat, then use a palette knife to cut it into the desired shapes. Then bevel the edges along each of the bottle's sides and the two end pieces, using a length of wood with one edge cut off at a 45-degree angle.

4. With a potter's needle, score the areas where the base and sides will join. Prepare a bowl of soft stoneware clay to use as slip, then smear the first side with slip and mount it onto the base. Use a set square to check that the side is vertical. Mount the second side the same way. Smooth the insides of the joints and press a roll of clay in them to strengthen them.

5. Continue adding the remaining walls following the same method. With the same type of clay, throw the neck of the bottle and place it on the top, then use a potter's needle to mark around the perimeter of its base. Also smooth the areas where the outside edges of the bottle join.

6. Make a hole in the top of the bottle the same size as the internal diameter of the neck you have thrown. Using a potter's needle, score from the hole to the circumference that you marked in the previous step, and also score the bottom of the neck. Smear them with slip and stick them together. Score around the area where the neck joins the bottle and add a roll of clay, pressing it down with a wooden knife. Finally, smooth the surface.

7. The glazed bottle looks like this.

Bottle, 1998. 14 3/4 x 3 x 3 in. (37.5 x 7.5 x 7.5 cm). Firing temperature: 2300°F (1260°C).

PADDLING

This method allows you to shape pieces modeled by hand and to change the shape of thrown pieces. The former method is more often used, particularly with pieces made from rolls or strips or shaped from solid blocks of clay. A paddle is used to smooth the walls and strengthen the joins, and at the same time the surface is textured.

There are no specific tools for this method, although it is a good idea to use materials such as wood, which does not stick to the clay because it is porous. A piece

of wood can also be utilized to create different textures, using either the flat face, the top, or the edges. You can also engrave textures on other tools; by hitting the damp clay with the carved wood, the imprints will be transferred.

The construction of this bottle with a modeled body and thrown necks should not present any difficulties. Using the wood to paddle the piece requires precision and care to avoid deforming it, unless you are deliberately aiming for this effect when you paddle it.

1. Shape the body of the vase using a block of earthenware clay with medium-grained grog; use a trimming tool to hollow it out. Paddle it with a wooden paddle until you have the shape you want.

2. Place one hand inside the piece to support the sides and prevent it from becoming deformed while you paddle it with the side of the wood to add texture.

3. Prepare the lid of the vase. Use a potter's needle to score the area where it is joined to the vase, and fold the edges so that they flap over.

4. Smear the top edges of the vase and the lid with slip.

5. Paddle the lid so that it sticks to the jar. The air inside ensures that the piece does not lose its shape.

6. Throw smooth necks, which will contrast with the paddled texture of the surface. Score the bottom edges of the necks and smear them with slip. Use a round cutter to pierce the top slab of clay, and place the necks on it.

7–8. The vase looks like this after modeling and after firing.

Vase, 1998. 14$^{1}/_{4}$ x 6 x 4$^{3}/_{4}$ in.
(36 x 15 x 12cm).
Firing temperature: 2300°F (1260°C).

INSCRIBING

*T*he most useful tool for this decoration is a potter's needle, although you can also use any other modeling tool that has a very fine blade. With the potter's needle, the incised pattern will have small specks of clay in it that are produced when the needle moves through the clay. Other tools will yield incisions with cleaner lines. For each design, use the particular tool best suited to marking the necessary incisions.

If you are working free-hand without an initial design, it is useful to practice on another surface of clay until your gestures flow. Remember that you are not simply drawing but that the tool is digging in and has to produce a small furrow in the clay.

The small specks of clay that are produced by the point of the tool can be left, or can be removed when the piece is dry, using fine sandpaper. Next, use a brush to clean the dust from the incisions. This decoration can be covered with a very light-colored transparent glaze, which will accumulate in the inscribed designs and thus highlight them. Opaque glazes are best avoided because they will cover up the incising. The piece can also be left unglazed, as in the following example.

1. Prepare a ⁵/₈-inch-thick (17 mm) slab of clay with medium-grained grog.

2. Cover the clay with plastic and place the full-sized design pattern on top of it.

3. Secure the pattern to the plastic with adhesive tape, then trace over the design with a hard pencil, using a hand rest to support your hand. Use a ruler to mark any straight lines in the design.

4. The drawing looks like this on the slab of clay.

5. Go over the drawing again with a potter's needle, this time making incisions in the clay. Use the hand rest during this process as well.

6. When you have finished inscribing the drawing, use the same tool to mark the shading in the design.

7. Cut along the base of the piece and leave the natural outline of the other three sides. This is how the finished piece looks during drying.

Still Life, 1998. 26³/₄ x 8¹/₄ x 6 in. (68 x 21 x 15 cm). Firing temperature: 2306°F (1280°C).

8. After the bisque firing I covered the surface of the mural with iron oxide dissolved in water, which is absorbed by the clay. Next, I washed it with a damp sponge to remove excess iron oxide from the surface, emphasizing the iron oxide that has penetrated into the incised drawing.

AGATE

*T*his process consists of mixing two or more different-colored clays. Don't overwork the clay, since too much mixing will homogenize the color too much and will not yield the proper marbling effect. The clay can be mixed by kneading or by placing alternating slabs on top of one another. The results can be very precise, according to the skill with which the clay is mixed, or can be left to chance, which produces very spectacular effects. The marbled clay can then be used with any system of modeling: pinching, coiling, strips, slabs, or throwing.

For shaping this bottle, I have mixed red clay with china clay and then cut the clay into slabs. Then I rolled and stretched it with a rolling pin to obtain the four sides of the vase, which are each somewhat different but complement one another. The piece is covered with a transparent colored glaze that highlights the pattern.

1. Using nylon wire and two ³/₈-inch (1cm) slats, cut blocks of red clay and china clay into slabs. Place the two slats so that they converge toward you, so they don't slip forward as you cut.

2. Pile up the slabs, alternating colors.

3. Knead the clay until you have a compact block, but don't mix it into a homogenous mass.

4. Cut the clay into slabs again as in step 2, and then use two 3/8-inch (8 mm) slats to make slabs that will form the walls of the vase. Cut them to the required size.

5. Let the clay dry so that the walls keep their shape while you model the vessel. Bevel the edges at a 45-degree angle so that the design fits together perfectly along each edge. I have used red clay slip here since this is the predominant color, but china clay slip can also be used.

6. I made the upper part of the vessel from four small slabs of clay. When the piece is finished, you can go over the surface with a flat tool to sharpen the pattern.

7. The finished vase has a transparent glaze on the outside and brilliant white on the inside.

Vase, 1998.
13³/₄ x 4¹/₂ x 4¹/₂ in.
(35 x 11.5 x 11.5 cm). Firing
temperature: 1760°F (960°C).

AGATE PASTE

A variation on this process is the use of highly contrasting colored clays. Unless you are trying to obtain a chance effect, it is best to prepare different colors using the same type of clay to prevent different levels of contraction during drying and firing, which could ruin the piece.

For this piece I prepared a porcelain clay, adding colored oxides when the clay was in powdered form so that they mixed uniformly.

The pieces made using this system can be low or high temperature. In the former case, it is useful to apply a transparent glaze, which will increase the chromatic effect, since otherwise the colors will be very dull (like pastels). In the latter case this is optional. The colors become more intense at high temperatures, so they can either be left as they are when they come out of the kiln, or they can be glazed, which will make the color even more intense.

1. Prepare eight blocks of colored clay using powdered porcelain and metal oxides (chrome, manganese, iron, and cobalt, from 1 to 3 percent).

2. Stick a roll of clay colored with cobalt oxide onto a small slab of white porcelain that you have moistened. You can also stick it on with slip made from the same material, either white or colored. Roll up the slab.

3. Follow the same process with the different-colored clays. Then cut the rolls into sections, putting them on a piece of plastic so that they do not dry out.

4. It is a good idea to prepare all the pieces at once that you might need. Cover a plastic bowl in cloth to use as a mold; place the disks inside it, sticking them close together and joining with water.

5. The bowl completely covered in colored clay.

6. Scrape a semi-circular rib over the inside of the bowl to mix the clay and smooth the surface. Leave the piece inside the mold until it is leather-hard. Meanwhile, prepare the base of the bowl in the same way.

7. The bowl during drying.

8. When the piece has been bisque-fired, apply a transparent glaze and then fire it again.

Bowl, 1998. 4 x 6³/₄ in. (10 x 16 cm). Firing temperature: 2336°F (1280°C).

PREPARING EGYPTIAN PASTE

The distinguishing characteristic of Egyptian paste is that after firing it is covered with a natural glaze thanks to soluble sodium salts. The oldest pieces made using this type of paste go back to about 5000 B.C.

There are three basic components of these pastes: silica, clay, and alkalis. The firing temperature for Egyptian paste is around 1742°F (950°C). This is the formula that I use:

Sodium feldspar	35%
Silicon	35%
Kaolin	13%
Sodium carbonate	7%
Sodium bicarbonate	6%
Bentonite	4%

Other formulas are:

Sodium feldspar	38%
Silicon	20%
Kaolin	15%
Sodium carbonate	10%
Sodium bicarbonate	7%
Ball clay	5%
Calcium carbonate	5%

Sodium feldspar	40%
Silicon	25%
Kaolin	15%
Sodium carbonate	10%
Sodium bicarbonate	6%
Bentonite	4%

Sodium feldspar	35%
Red clay	28%
Silicon	20%
Sodium carbonate	10%
Sodium bicarbonate	5%
Bentonite	2%

When preparing these clays, the amount of water must be carefully adjusted because too much water will dilute the soluble sodium salts. First the carbonate and bicarbonate are dissolved in water, and the remaining ingredients are mixed together dry and then added.

This is a very inelastic paste, so modeling can be laborious and large pieces are not practical. To increase its elasticity, elastic clays such as ball clay and bentonite are added to the formula.

Small pieces can be modeled from solid blocks, but it cannot be used to build in slabs unless it is fitted into a mold, which should be covered with a fine cloth. If the clay touches the surface of the mold, when the salts rise to the surface they will corrode it. An alternative method is to use terracotta molds.

This clay should be shaped quickly, then place the pieces on a ceramic tray covered with burnt aluminum oxide on which they can be dried and fired. The pieces must be handled with care; do not touch them with your fingers, to avoid dislodging the soluble salts that rise to the surface in dust and crystal form (this will become the glaze).

The resultant colors are obtained from the following materials, in the following proportions. A higher percentage of oxide produces darker, more metallic colors:

Copper carbonate ($CuCO3$): 1–3% = turquoise
Copper oxide ($Cu_2 O$): 0.25–1% = turquoise
Cobalt oxide ($CO_2 O_3$): 0.25–1% = blue
Cobalt carbonate ($CO CO_3$): 1–3% = blue
Iron oxide ($Fe_2 O_3$): 1–10% = pink, salmon
Manganese dioxide ($Mn O_2$): 0.25–2% = purple
Chrome oxide ($Cr_2 O_3$): 1–7 % = yellowish green

1. I prepared 13 pounds (6kg) of powdered clay according to the first formula, which I then divided into portions of 1/2 pound (200g) each, to which I added different percentages of metallic oxides.

2. Using a mortar and pestle I mixed the dry powder with the oxide. I placed 34 ounces (100cl) of water in each plastic container and then added the powdered mixture. When the mixture settles, it can be stirred with a rubber spatula.

3. I let the mixtures stand for 48 hours, with the receptacles covered in plastic to prevent the water from evaporating. I prepared six small wooden frames on a plaster tray, with a cloth in each one, and added each of the prepared mixtures to them. The cloth prevents the mixture from combining with particles of plaster.

4. The plaster tray corroded by the alkalis in the mixtures.

5. When the plaster has absorbed all the surplus water, some of the sample mixtures look like this once they have achieved the correct consistency. The mixtures should be put into plastic bags to keep them from drying out.

6. I have engraved a small motif on a plaster tablet, basing it on Egyptian designs. I stamped it onto a slab of clay 1/4 inch (7 mm) thick and then cut it out with a rectangular cutter. Next I engraved six more motifs for each set of three samples.

7–12. During drying the samples are placed on ceramic trays covered in aluminum oxide so that they do not stick during firing. The same samples after firing measure 2^7/8 x 2^1/8 x ^{1}/4 inches (7.3 x 5.5 x 0.7 cm). I have raised the percentages of oxides to show the resulting colors.

8.
A. Copper carbonate 3, 5, 7%
B. Manganese dioxide: 2, 5, 8%
C. Cobalt carbonate 3, 5, 7%

10.
A. Iron oxide: 3, 7, 10%
B. Copper oxide: 1, 3, 5%

12.
A. Chrome oxide: 3, 5, 7%
B. Cobalt oxide: 1, 3, 5%

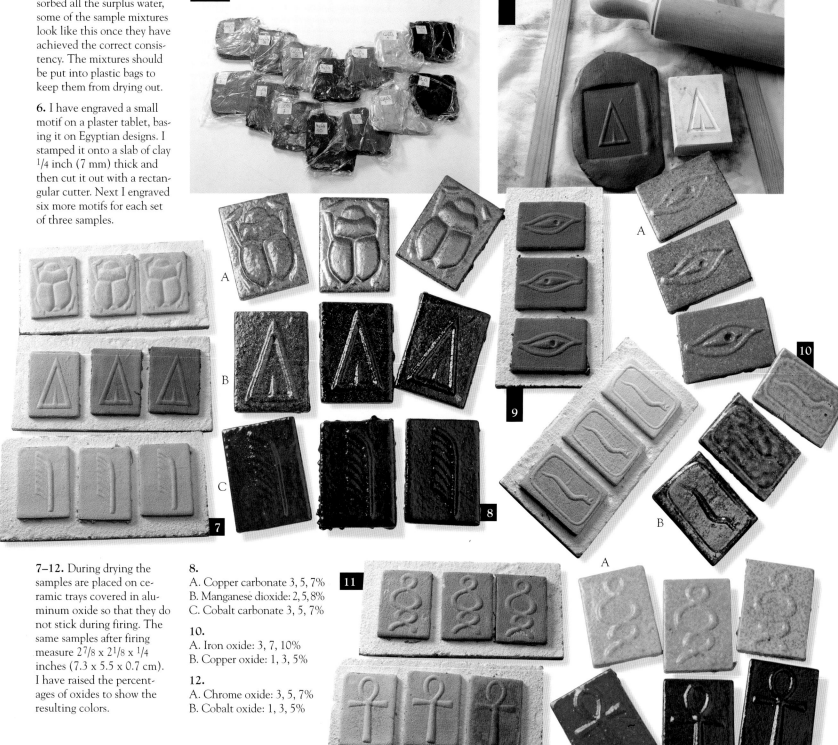

SCULPTURES USING EGYPTIAN PASTE

*T*o make this small sculpture, I prepared 4 1/2 pounds (2kg) of clay with 5 percent copper carbonate. In the other pieces I used colored clay left over from the samples mixed in the previous chapter. The results were as expected, considering that I had already fired the samples.

The pyramidal stump form with imprinted relief was sculpted from a block; the other pieces were made by pinching, using various "molds" such as a bisque-fired clay bowl, a plastic receptacle (square bowl), a plastic tube (cylinder), and a cardboard box (prism). The firing temperature for all the pieces was 1760°F (960°C).

1. Place the clay on a plaster tray, following the same process as in the samples.

2. These are the materials and tools necessary to make the sculpture: clay, open mold, cloth, and two clamps.

3. Close the mold, place pieces of wood on each side, and tighten the clamps. This allows the pressure of the clamps to be supported by the wood and prevents the plaster from breaking. Stretch out the cloth inside the mold so that the clay does not touch the plaster directly, and then fill it using the pinch method.

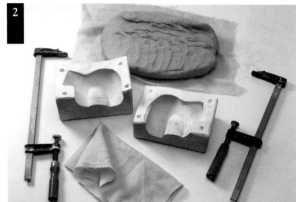

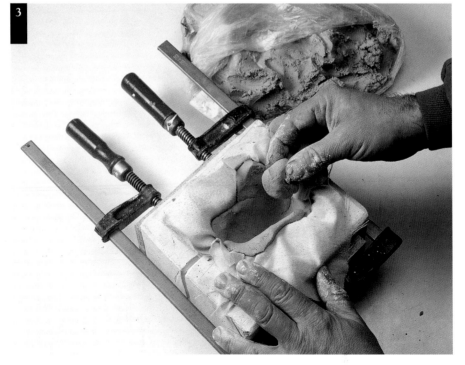

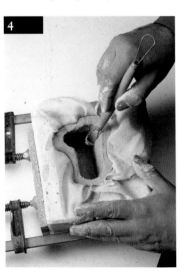

4. When it is full, smooth the inside and the base with a trimming tool.

5. While the clay hardens inside the mold, prepare the board on which the piece will stand during drying and firing by dusting it with aluminum hydrate.

6–7. The piece after drying and after firing.

Hippopotamus, 1998.
5 x 3 1/8 x 3 1/8 in.
(13 x 8.5 x 8 cm).

8. To demonstrate different methods I molded a pyramidal trunk form on which I stamped four motifs. As in the previous exercise, after making the piece I placed it on a stand covered with aluminum.

9. Detail of the alkali surface that the glaze forms during firing.

10. The piece after firing.

Prism, 1998.
5 1/2 x 2 3/8 x 2 3/8 in.
(14 x 6 x 6 cm).

Prism, 1998.
4 3/8 x 2 1/8 x 2 in.
(11 x 5.5 x 5 cm).

Cylinder, 1998. 3 3/8 x 2
in. (8.5 x 5 cm).

Bowl, 1998. 2 3/8 x 4 3/4 in.
(6.5 x 12 cm).

Rectangular Bowl, 1998.
4 1/2 x 4 x 2 1/8 in.
(11.5 x 10 x 5.5 cm).

11. These four pieces were modeled by mixing clays together. Different-shaped objects have been used as molds.

12. The pieces after firing.

EGYPTIAN PASTE JEWELRY

*T*his paste is ideal for making jewelry since it glazes itself and thus requires only one firing. Each piece should be a suitable form and size for its function (beads, pendants, bracelets, chokers, earrings, and so on).

No special tools are required; if you wish to make a series of pieces, prepare small molds and stamps. In this case it is better to use terra-cotta than plaster.

The design of the pieces will depend individual preference; the possibilities are endless. After the pieces are removed from the kiln they can be set or glued into metal settings, which are sold in stores that carry jewelry findings. Nylon thread can also be used for necklaces and leather can be used for pendants, or a jeweler can set the clay into precious metals such as gold, silver, or platinum.

1–2. To make the smaller pieces I used small metal cutters. For the others I stamped the decorative motifs with different plastic objects. This is what the pieces look like when they come out of the kiln.

3–4. Beads can be made from molded rolls that are then cut up and a hole inserted with a potter's needle, or they can be made from little balls that, like the other pieces, are placed on a tray of aluminum. Notice the difference in color between the dry beads and the fired ones.

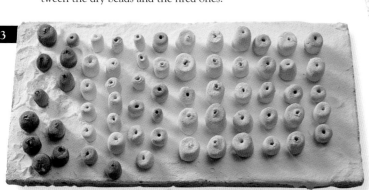

5. To make these quadrilateral pendants I paddled three slabs of clay, then cut them out with a cutter and made holes in the top with a potter's needle. For the small pendant and the earrings I stamped the clay with two small plaster molds.

6–8. The pieces after firing at 1760°F (960°C).

Earrings, 1998.
2³/₄ x ¹/₂ x ¹/₈ in.
(7 x 1.2 x 0.5 cm).

Pendant, 1998.
3¹/₂ x 1¹/₈ x ¹/₈ in.
(9 x 3 x 0.5 cm).

Pendant, 1998. 4¹/₈ x 2³/₈ x ¹/₈ in.
(10.5 x 6 x 0.5 cm).

Pendant, 1998. 8¹/₄ x 2³/₈ x ¹/₈ in.
(21 x 6 x 0.5 cm).

9–10. The pectoral was prepared using clays with iron oxide and copper carbonate and was paddled, while the pendant was stamped, leaving the outline produced by pressing the mold onto the clay. For this pendant I mixed two clays with cobalt oxide. These are the two pieces after firing at 1760°F (960°C).

Pectoral, 1998.
7⁷/₈ x 3¹/₂ x ¹/₈ in.
(20 x 9 x 0.5 cm).

Pendant, 1998.
4 ¹/₂ x 2³/₄ x ¹/₈ in.
(11.5 x 7 x 0.5 cm).

11–12. The bracelet is fairly complex, since I made various rolls of clay with different oxides and joined them together by pressing them down with a rolling pin supported by ¹/₄-inch (7 mm) slats. Then I shaped the bracelet over a cardboard tube covered with a cloth, and left it to dry there. Before placing the piece in the kiln, I removed it from the cardboard tube, without touching the cloth, and placed it on a tray of aluminum. Then I removed the cloth with tongs and fired the piece at 1760°F (960°C). Here you can see the different colors created by the various oxides.

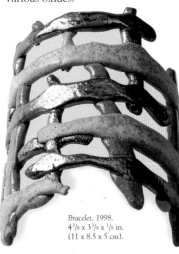

Bracelet, 1998.
4³/₈ x 3³/₈ x ¹/₈ in.
(11 x 8.5 x 5 cm).

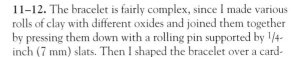
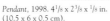

DECORATING LEATHER-HARD PIECES
FLUTING

*T*his method is used for making grooves or furrows on the surfaces of thrown pieces. They can be made on soft, damp pieces or on leather-hard ones; normal ceramics tools are used, such as trimming tools, although wooden knives can also be used. After making each groove it is a good idea to clean the tool to remove any particles of clay that are stuck to it, which might blur or misshape the next groove. The small specks of clay that the tool leaves behind can be left on the piece or can be removed with fine sand-paper after drying and before bisque-firing.

The best forms for this process are those with straight sides or thrown cylinders. Making grooves in other thrown pieces is difficult, although it can be achieved with practice. It is preferable to use fine clays, with grog that is imperceptible or fine. The glaze highlights the grooves, gathering more thickly in the hollows, while only a fine layer of glaze is left on the tops of the ridges.

1. First throw a vase using stoneware with fine grog. Polish it, then use a potter's needle to mark two parallel lines, between which the grooves will be dug out. Prepare a cardboard set square to act as a guide for marking the grooves. Support the handle of a round trimming tool against the hypotenuse of the set square so that all the grooves run at the same angle, are parallel, and at the same distance from one another. The grooves are about 1/8-inch (4 mm) deep.

2–3. The grooved vase while drying and after glaze firing.

Vase, 1998. 6³/8 x 5 in. (17.5 x 13 cm). Firing temperature: 2300°F (1260°C).

Receptacle, 1998. 7 x 6¹/4 in. (18 x 16 cm). Firing temperature: 2300°F (1260°C).

4. Another fluting process consists of working directly on a freshly thrown piece before removing it from the wheel. Using a potter's needle, mark the lines between which the grooves will be dug out. In this case I used a plastic set square, using one of the vertical sides to mark the space between the grooves and also to support the round edge of the wide trimming tool that digs them out.

5. Remove the piece from the wheel and leave it to harden. Throw three small cylinders to use as the feet of the pot, and make grooves in them as well. When the piece reaches leather-hardness, polish the four parts of the piece, and join them together with slip.

6. The finished piece after the glaze firing.

FACETING

This is a creative process that is generally used for thrown pieces. It can be done in two ways: either straight after throwing, when the clay is soft, or after waiting until the clay is leather-hard. These thrown pieces should have thicker walls so that when you cut all the facets the thickness of the clay will be as regular as possible, and so that the piece does not crack during drying or firing.

The tools for making each facet are simple. For soft pieces, it is best to use a fine wire, which will not stick during cutting (a problem that would occur if a knife or a rib were used, since their blades are fine but wide). But for leather-hard pieces, a sharp knife is ideal.

Before making a piece with this technique, calculate the facets so they will fit exactly within the perimeter and the first and the last ones will meet.

1. Throw a stoneware bowl and a cylinder. On a piece of stiff paper, draw two circles with the same diameters as the pieces. Then draw hexagons over the circles. Turn these into dodecahedrons by drawing the perpendicular bisectors of each side. Cut them out.

2. Place the polygonal pieces of paper over the center of the bowl and the cylinder, and use the potter's needle to mark the lines of each cut.

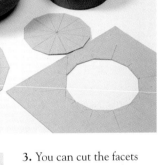

3. You can cut the facets with any cutting implement. In this case I used a knife blade, which I rested along the line to be cut, ensuring that the facet lay within the lines I had marked.

4. The two faceted parts before they are joined.

5–6. Continue by scoring the areas of the join, and smear them with slip. After joining them, push a roll of clay into the join to reinforce it. Use the potter's needle to make a hole in the base so that the air can escape.

7–8. The cup while it is drying and after is has been glazed.

Cup, 1998. 3³/₄ x 7¹/₂ in. (9.5 x 19.5 cm). Firing temperature: 2300°F (1260°C).

OPENWORK, PART 1

For this decorative piece, the walls of the piece are perforated, or fretted, when they are leather-hard. The tools required are sharp metal modeling tools, knife blades, scalpels, cutters, and a potter's needle.

Before beginning an openwork piece, it is important to plan ahead and to have a clear idea of the design you want to cut and the tools you will need to cut it, since once you have made the perforations you can't go change your mind. It is also important to leave sufficient distance between each hole so the clay between them does not break.

Openwork can be improvised or made with the help of templates whose design is marked with a potter's needle before making the cuts. Using the potter's needle you can also make very fine holes, and if a transparent glaze is used to cover them (even a colored one), when the light shines through them it will create a translucent effect.

In these exercises I have made two types of openwork, one cutting from the outside, the other cutting from the inside, as explained below.

1. Mold a porcelain bowl in the form of a cone by using a funnel lined with a cloth. This texture will be imprinted onto the outside of the piece. For the openwork use cylindrical cutters. Since it is an open shape, you can make the perforations from the inside. Using the cutter, begin to make holes in the piece and continue the process with other cutters of different sizes until the openwork is complete.

2. When the openwork is done, prepare the parts that will form the base of the cup and join them to the body.

3. The finished piece after glazing and firing.

Cup, 1998.
5³/₈ x 6¹/₄ in. (13.5 x 16 cm).
Firing temperature: 2336°F (1280°C).

4. Roll out a slab of porcelain on a piece of coarsely textured cotton and wrap it around a cardboard tube covered in newspaper. With a potter's needle, score the end that makes the join and smear it with slip. Do the same with the part of the slab that flaps over it. Prepare another small slab of clay to act as the base, place the cylinder on it, and join them together. Leave the piece to harden, then with a length of thread mark the area to be cut. Using a metal modeling tool, cut out triangles on both sides of the thread to make a zig-zag relief. This openwork can be done without removing the cardboard tube, which helps to preserve the piece's shape.

5. When the openwork is complete, remove the cardboard tube so that the piece does not break as it dries, but leave the newspaper in place to act as a support. Remove the paper when the piece is leather-hard.

6. The piece when it has been glazed and fired.

Cylinder, 1998.
12¹/₄ x 3¹/₈ in. (31 x 8).
Firing temperature: 2336°F (1280°C).

OPENWORK, PART 2

Another way of doing openwork is to utilize a piece with double walls, a method much used in previous centuries.

In this exercise I have made an incense holder using two concentric bowls that are joined only at the top. The design allows the bowl to be held in the hands without burning them, even though the inner bowl might get very hot.

1. For this piece, model two concentric hemispherical bowls, which will be joined by a base so that when the piece has been fretted it will have the shape of a circular crown. Score and slip the areas where the pieces join and stick them together, leaving the piece upside down until it is leather-hard, so that the bowl inside does not become unstuck.

2. Cut out two slabs of clay, 3/8 inch (1 cm) thick, which will slot into each other and whose top will be the same shape as the base of the bowl. Stand the base on the bowl and use a potter's needle to mark and score where it will join.

3. With the potter's needle, draw in the areas that will be fretted, and use a scalpel to fret them, making sure that none of the pieces of clay fall inside.

4. Detail of the fretted bowl.

5. When the openwork is finished, join the two parts of the incense holder.

6. The finished piece.

Incense holder, 1998. 6⁷/₈ x 6³/₄ in. (17.5 x 17 cm). Firing temperature: 2300°F (1260°C).

CARVING

Carving is a system of decoration applied to leather-hard pieces. It can be used for any kind of ceramic work, although on concave pieces (plates, vases, bowls) you should avoid reliefs that are too deep or hollow since a buildup of unnecessary glaze can form there and create bubbles or even cover the carved motifs entirely. With vertical pieces such as jugs and sculptures this depth is not a problem, since the verticality tends to distribute all the glaze evenly.

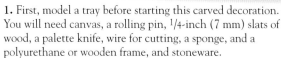

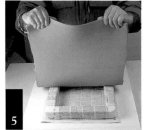

1. First, model a tray before starting this carved decoration. You will need canvas, a rolling pin, 1/4-inch (7 mm) slats of wood, a palette knife, wire for cutting, a sponge, and a polyurethane or wooden frame, and stoneware.

2. Press the rolls of clay onto the canvas and join them together by pressing down with both thumbs facing in opposite directions.

3. Roll the rolling pin over them to make a slab.

4. If the slab sticks to the canvas, or when you roll the rolling pin over it it does not stretch, it is useful to lift the clay up off the canvas; then put it back in its place and roll the rolling pin over it again. The slab should stretch out and even up perfectly.

5. When the slab is ready, lift it by one end and place it on the frame, allowing it to spread over the edges.

6. The weight of the slab itself will make it fit to the shape of the frame. Pass a damp sponge over it, pressing down the surface of the slab carefully to make it adapt to the right shape.

7. Use the spatula to go around the frame and cut off the excess clay.

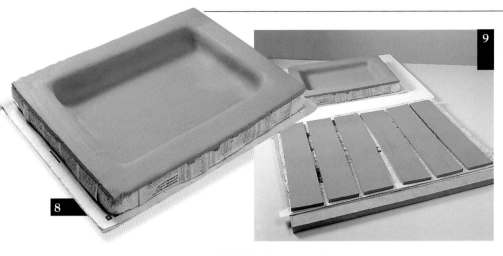

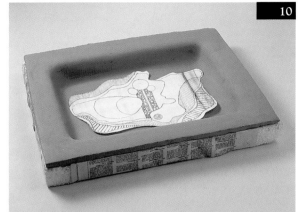

8. The tray is now finished.

9. Model some strips of clay to be used later for the support or legs of the tray. Let them dry along with the tray until everything is leather-hard.

10. Place a photocopy of the drawing you want to carve in the bottom of the tray.

11. In order to avoid touching the surface of the tray, work with a wooden hand rest supported on two pieces of wood. Trace over the outlines of the drawing with a potter's needle.

12. When the tracing is done, lift up the photocopy carefully, checking that all the lines have been clearly marked.

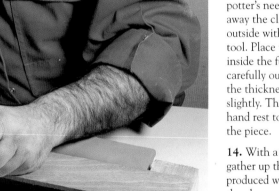

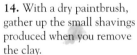

13. Go over the lines with a potter's needle, then carve away the clay around the outside with a fine modeling tool. Place the wooden knife inside the furrow and draw it carefully outward, to reduce the thickness of the surface slightly. Throughout use a hand rest to avoid touching the piece.

14. With a dry paintbrush, gather up the small shavings produced when you remove the clay.

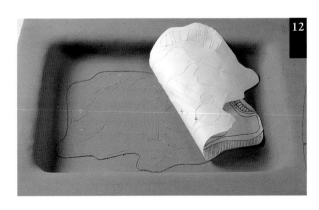

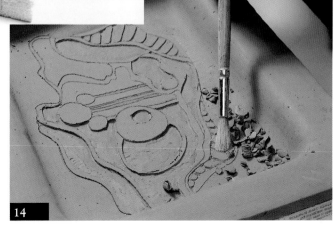

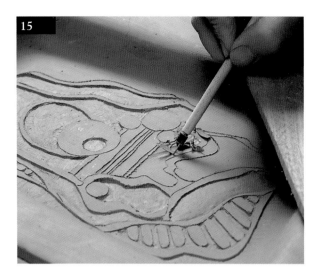

18. Take the strips of clay prepared at the beginning and shape the legs of the tray, marking the perimeter of the base and the excess clay of the legs with a potter's needle.

19. Cut the excess clay from the legs using a metal modeling tool.

20. With the potter's needle, score the tray base and the corresponding section of leg.

21. Smear the scored areas with slip; stick legs in place.

22. Smooth the joints and press a roll of clay along the outside.

15. Use a trimming tool to reduce the clay on the inside surface of the drawn motif.

16. Go over the design surface with a small, square-ended stick to smooth it.

17. Draw on the edge of the frame with a potter's needle, linking the design to the central motif. With a small, cylindrical-ended stick, imprint small circles of differing depth on the surface.

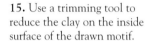
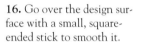

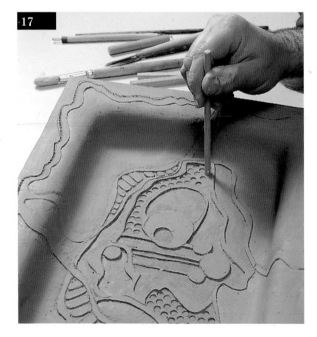

23. When all the strips that form the legs have been attached, place a roll of clay along their inner angle so that they stick firmly to the base of the tray.

24. The finished tray, upside down.

25. Place the tray inside the frame, so that it is supported by the top edge. Use the metal modeling tool to cut along the top, following the outline that you drew earlier.

26–27. Three-quarter view of the finished tray, seen from above.

28. The tray after bisque-firing.

29. The tray after glazing.

Organic, 1997.
Slab-built stoneware with carved motif,
$13^{1}/_{8}$ x $10^{1}/_{4}$ x $3^{1}/_{8}$ in. (34 x 26 x 8 cm).
Firing temperature: 2336°F (1280°C).

CLOISONNÉ

*B*ased on the art of enameling, this decorative method is only used on flat surfaces. The technique entails keeping the glaze within a network of small partitions that form part of the design of the piece; they are shaped with rolls of clay or, as in this exercise, with fine strips that are attached to the surface of the piece with slip. These strips or rolls can be prepared using the same clay as the rest of the piece, but colored with oxide, or they can be left the natural color of the clay.

After bisque-firing the piece, the glazes are applied to the spaces using a paintbrush or a bulb. The partitions stop the glazes from mixing.

1. Using stoneware with fine-grained grog, roll out a slab of clay $1/2$ inch (14 mm) thick, and various strips clay $1/8$ inch (3 mm) thick for the cloisonné. Place a fine sheet of transparent plastic over the slab of clay and place the design on top of the plastic.

2. Go over the drawing with a hard pencil, using a ruler for any straight lines.

3. The slab of clay with the drawing inscribed on it.

4. Using a potter's needle, score the areas where the strips will be attached, and which will form the cloisonné.

5. On the $1/8$-inch (3 mm) strips of clay, draw the design again and cut it out with a metal modeling tool.

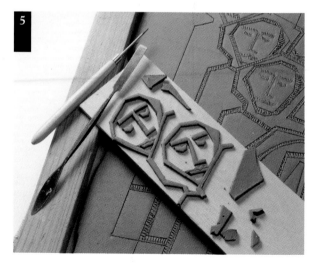

6. Smear slip on the areas where the strips will be attached, and attach the strips that you have cut out.

7. After making the cloisonné, use a palette knife to cut along the outer border.

8. The piece cut out and in the process of drying.

9. Once you have bisque-fired the piece, prepare the glazes to fill the areas delineated by the cloisonné.

10. When applying the glaze, it is important to avoid getting it on the partitions dividing the different areas.

11–12. The glazed mural before and after firing.

Mural, 1998.
13³/₄ x 8¹/₄ x ¹/₂ in. (35 x 21 x 1.3 cm).
Firing temperature: 2300°F (1260°C).

RELIEF

With leather-hard pieces it is possible to attach pinches, rolls, strips, and even slabs of the same clay, colored or otherwise, using slip. It is even possible to change the shape of the piece. It is also possible to model the piece itself directly, but keep in mind how thick the clay is in the areas that are being modeled, since they will have to be hollowed out if the relief is too pronounced. For this hollowing out, make holes to allow the air to circulate and to prevent the piece from exploding during firing, when the volume of warm air contained within it expands. These holes must connect with the interior or exterior of the piece, which should have a general ventilation hole.

1. Throw a stoneware vase, polish it, and let it harden. Prepare the motif you are going to make in relief on a strip of paper whose length is the same as the perimeter of the vase.

2. Transfer the design from the paper to a slab of stoneware 3/16 inch (5 mm) thick.

3. Before it reaches leather-hardness, cut the drawing out of the clay with a metal modeling tool.

4. Make two parallel lines to mark the relief area. Score the whole area and the underside of the relief.

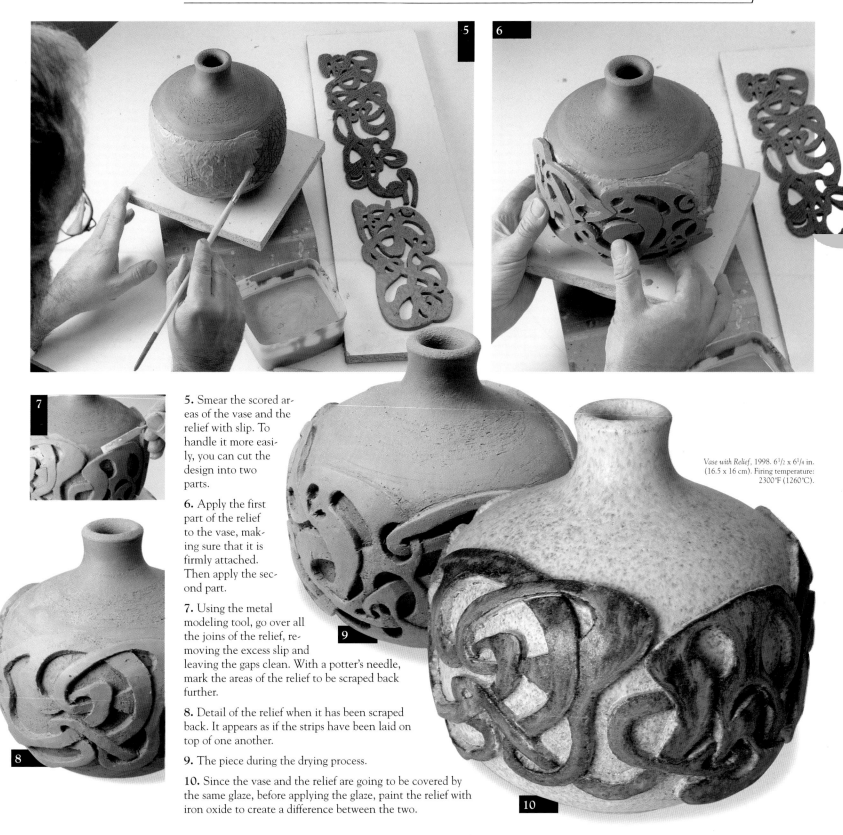

5. Smear the scored areas of the vase and the relief with slip. To handle it more easily, you can cut the design into two parts.

6. Apply the first part of the relief to the vase, making sure that it is firmly attached. Then apply the second part.

7. Using the metal modeling tool, go over all the joins of the relief, removing the excess slip and leaving the gaps clean. With a potter's needle, mark the areas of the relief to be scraped back further.

8. Detail of the relief when it has been scraped back. It appears as if the strips have been laid on top of one another.

9. The piece during the drying process.

10. Since the vase and the relief are going to be covered by the same glaze, before applying the glaze, paint the relief with iron oxide to create a difference between the two.

Vase with Relief, 1998. 6^1/$_2$ x 6^1/$_4$ in. (16.5 x 16 cm). Firing temperature: 2300°F (1260°C).

REPEATED RELIEF

*T*his relief can be applied to leather-hard pieces to form repeated patterns. Generally small, they are prepared using molds that can be made in two ways. One way is to model the design with clay, then cast plaster over it. The other way, which is used here, is to carve the negative of the image out of plaster.

In the first case, the mold is filled with clay, the excess clay is removed, and the motif is removed from the mold using a ball of the same clay. In the second case, a slab of clay of appropriate thickness is prepared and the mold is pressed down on it. The pressure makes the clay fill the mold, and when the mold is removed, it leaves the motif in relief. The motif can then be cut out when the clay has reached leather-hardness. After scoring the back of the motif and the surface of the piece where it is going to be stuck on, it is joined using slip. The clay for these motifs can be colored, which will make them contrast with the body of the piece.

1. Throw a cylinder using stoneware and draw the motifs you want to apply to it.

2. Trace the motifs of the relief on two plaster forms.

3. Using a potter's needle, go over the design traced on the plaster, and then engrave it using a metal modeling tool.

4. Detail of the engraved stamps, the designs, and the necessary tools.

5. Prepare a slab of clay ¹/4 inch (6 mm) thick and place it over the mold, pushing it down so that the relief is well defined.

6. The relief stamped onto the clay, and the mold.

7. With a spatula or a modeling tool, cut along the outside edges of each relief.

8. Detail of the cut-out motifs ready to be applied to the cylinder. You must wait until both the motifs and the cylinder reach leather-hardness before applying them.

9. Score the piece where each piece of the relief is going to be applied and score the back of each one. Smear the joins with slip and stick them on.

10. The finished piece, showing how the patterns of the relief have been alternated.

11. The glazed and fired cylinder.

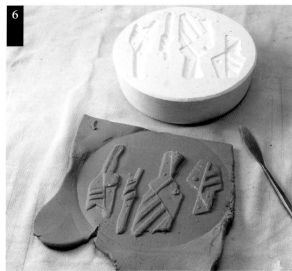

Cylinder, 1998.
10¹/4 x 5³/4 in. (26 x 14.5 cm).
Firing temperature: 2300°F (1260°C).

PREPARING ENGOBES

Engobes are creamy solutions of clay applied to damp, unfired pieces of a different color. Engobes can be white or colored with oxides and pigments. They can be fired at high or low temperatures depending on the components. These must be calculated for the type of clay to which they will be applied. In order to obtain a similar color to glazes, the proportion of colored oxides used with engobes needs to be higher. The ceramic pigments are applied in higher proportions to the oxides; otherwise the colors would turn pale.

After applying an engobe, the pieces need to be dried slowly; if necessary they can be covered with plastic to slow the drying process. Rapid drying produces cracks, and can also make the engobe come off, so it is important to calculate how the engobe will shrink and adjust it according to the clay being used for the piece. Pieces covered with engobe are fired like other pieces. Leave more space between them in the kiln so that the colors do not contaminate one another through possible volatilization of the oxides.

Unfired pieces can be decorated with engobes applied in different ways, as explained on the the following pages. Almost all the processes can be used in combination, so the decorative possibilities are endless.

1. To prepare 1³/4-ounce (50g) samples of engobes, weigh the ingredients (red clay 67 percent; kaolin 33 percent, to which 10 percent of flux is added). For each oxide, prepare four percentages (1, 3, 5, and 7 percent). Begin with copper carbonate, using precision scales to weigh it.

2. Place the engobe and the oxide in a mortar and grind them at length, until the mixture is homogenous. Remember that these mixtures must be mixed dry. Then add 17 ounces (50cl) of water to the engobe and continue stirring until it forms a smooth liquid, without any lumps. Repeat this process with each of the samples.

3. General view of some of the dry engobe samples, with the percentages of oxides and pigments on top, showing the different pigmentation. Next they will be mixed and water added, and then covered with plastic to keep them from evaporating or getting dirty.

4. I have prepared small tablets of red clay, 3¹/2 x 2 x ³/8 x inches (9 x 5 x 0.8 cm), which I have divided into four parts with incised lines, and with another line running across the bottom, where I will write the percentage of the oxide in each sample. Using a paintbrush, apply the engobe to the tablets, thickly enough for the color of the red clay of the tablet not to come through. Place the samples on a plastic grid that will allow them to dry uniformly, with both sides exposed to the air.

5. Engobe samples with metal oxides after the second firing; I added a transparent, shiny glaze. From left to right, top to bottom: white engobe, copper carbonate, chrome oxide, lead chromate, cobalt oxide, iron oxide, cobalt carbonate, iron chromate, manganese dioxide, and copper oxide.

6. These engobes were prepared with pigments. From left to right, top to bottom: carmine, yellow, blue, lilac, light green, black, brown, dark green, and emerald green. All these engobes have the same percentages of pigment: 3, 5, 8, and 10 percent, except black, which is 5, 8, 10, and 15 percent.

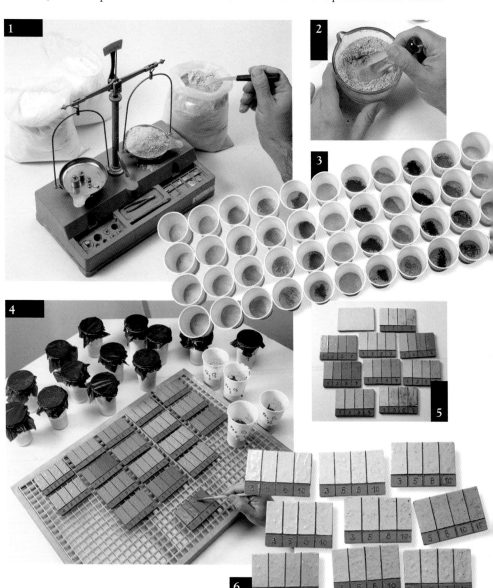

ENGOBES WITH A PAINTBRUSH

*W*hen applying an engobe with a paintbrush, the piece should be leather-hard and free from dust. If the decoration calls for it, the areas where the engobe will be applied can be delineated with a potter's needle.

The engobe must be liquid, so the paintbrush will flow over the surface; if it has thickened, stir in a little water.

Remember that an engobe that has not been used settles and forms sediment, so it must be stirred before use.

After applying the engobe, the piece must be dried very slowly.

1. To carry out this exercise, prepare a slab of red clay 3/8 inch (1 cm) thick. Shape it into a curve and stand it on a base of the same material. Use a metal knife to cut out the shape and add the decorative elements in relief.

2. After applying the parts in relief, use the potter's needle to draw the lines that separate the different colors of the engobes. The photograph shows samples of the engobes to be used for decorating the figure. To work on the piece, place it on a banding wheel to make it easier to apply the engobes to each side.

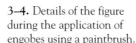

3–4. Details of the figure during the application of engobes using a paintbrush.

Figure, 1998.
13 1/8 x 5 1/2 x 4 1/2 in.
(33.5 x 14 x 11.5 cm).
Firing temperature:
1760°F (960°C).

5. After applying engobes to both sides of the figure, move on to the base to complete the piece.

6. The finished figure. To keep the arms from breaking once the engobe is dry to the touch, cover the whole piece with a cardboard box to slow down the drying process.

7–8. The two sides of the figure after firing.

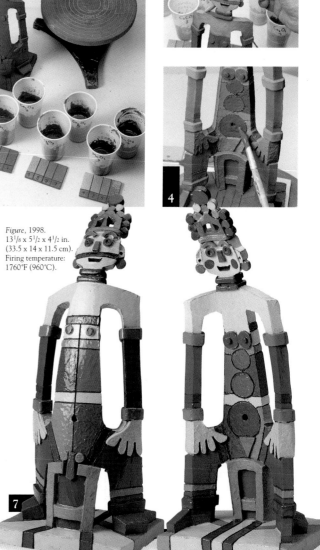

PAPER RESISTS

Resists are used for areas that are going to be left the natural color of the clay, and so are not covered with engobe. To make resists for the engobe, paper is cut out and dampened, which helps the paper stick to the piece. The strips of paper should be applied smoothly, without creases. The engobe is then applied to the parts that remain uncovered. The edges of the paper determine the outlines of the decoration, and the width of the resist will keep the engobes from mixing. When the paper is dry, which does not take long, the resist is carefully removed, making sure not to dislodge the engobe. The piece is then allowed to dry.

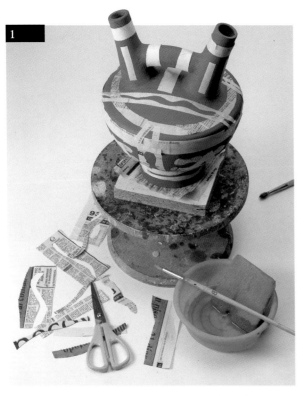

1. For this piece I have thrown a vase with two necks and a piece that links them. Cut out strips of newspaper in the pattern that will form the resist, dampen them, and put them in place on the piece.

2–3. Different engobes are applied in the spaces between the strips of paper.

4. When the engobe has dried to the touch, carefully remove the paper resists one by one, using a potter's needle to avoid damaging the piece.

5. The vase during drying.

6. When the vase has been bisque-fired, apply a transparent glaze to bring out the colors of the engobe.

Vase, 1998.
9¹/₄ x 7¹/₂ in.
(23.5 x 19 cm).
Firing temperature:
1760°F (960°C).

COMBING

Combing is an engobe decoration in which a tube or the quill of a feather is used to mix different-colored engobes either in parallel or at a different angle. The engobe is applied with a bulb, which will allow the lines to be thick and heavy. The quill is then drawn across the lines of engobe, mixing it slightly. The same result can be obtained with the point of a potter's needle or with the blade of a metal modeling tool, but the implement should not scratch or penetrate the piece, which could distort the design.

1. Modeled plate with engobes, bulbs for applying them, and a feather for combing.

2. Use a bulb to apply the first engobe, drawing parallel lines and leaving enough space between them for filling in other engobes. Continue applying the second engobe of iron oxide.

3. Use the quill of the feather to begin combing the engobe, drawing it perpendicularly across the previous lines, superimposing the new lines over the old ones.

4. Repeat the same process of applying engobes and combing along the borders of the plate.

5. The appearance of the decorated plate during drying.

6. After bisque-firing, apply a transparent glaze to the plate and fire it again. Notice that the cobalt oxide glaze is more dominant than the iron oxide, so the resultant color is blue.

Plate, 1998.
11 x 11 x 1¹/₂ in.
(28 x 28 x 4 cm).
Firing temperature:
2300°F (1260°C).

MARBLING

In this process, as in the previous one, engobes of different colors are applied with a bulb, this time to a concave surface. Then the piece is moved around with both hands so that the engobe mixes. This movement, brusque and sharp and from left to right, cre- *ates a jasperized or marbled effect, because it looks like the veining of these minerals. This way of applying engobes creates unique patterns that are always different and unpredictable since the movement of the gesture is different each time.*

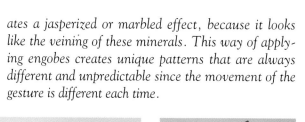

1. Model a slab of stoneware with medium-grained grog and place it over a bowl covered with a cloth, to give it a concave shape. Prepare a square of cardboard and place it over the bowl to act as a template for cutting out the shape you want. Also model the base of the piece using a slab of clay 4 inches (10 cm) wide, and roll it into a cylinder.

2. When the piece is leather-hard, place the two parts together without joining them, to check that they correspond with each other. They must be kept separate in order to marble the base. Then prepare three engobes: a white one, and two with iron oxide at 1 and 3 percent.

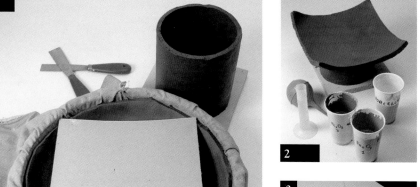

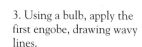

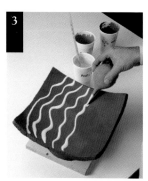

3. Using a bulb, apply the first engobe, drawing wavy lines.

4. Continue by applying the other two engobes.

5. Hold the piece in both hands and move it in different directions so that the engobes mix together to give the desired effect. To prevent the liquid in the engobes from deforming the piece, return it to the bowl, so that it will keep its shape until it has hardened. Repeat the process with the base.

6. Finally, when the two parts are leather-hard, join them together with slip. This is how the finished piece looks.

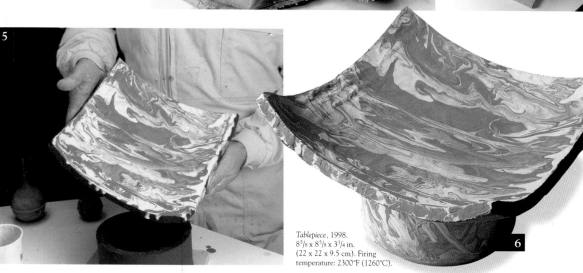

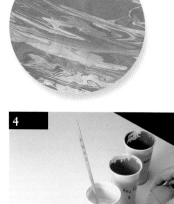

Tablepiece, 1998.
8⅝ x 8⅝ x 3¾ in.
(22 x 22 x 9.5 cm). Firing temperature: 2300°F (1260°C).

OXIDES USING ENGOBES

*T*his method of decoration is based on the application of oxides onto freshly applied engobe, except that these oxides must be dissolved water in which tobacco has been boiled. The result is the formation of a treelike or plantlike design in the engobe. The design will continue to expand while the engobe is still wet if more oxide is added to the base of the drawing. The decorations that result from using this method are always different.

1. Throw three cylinders of different sizes out of red clay, and polish them. Prepare a container full of engobe and dip them in.

2. The piece covered with engobe. Notice that a space has been left at the base, so that the piece can be held while it is being decorated.

3. Hold the piece pointing toward the floor and apply the iron oxide dissolved in tobacco water to the line of the engobe. Because the engobe is still wet, the solution flows downward, creating plantlike forms that grow as more solution is added and while the engobe is still wet.

4. Detail of one of the decorations.

5. The three cylinders when the decoration is complete.

6. After bisque-firing, apply a brilliant, opaque, white glaze to the inside of the cylinders and a brilliant, transparent glaze to the outside.

Cylinders, 1998.
5 3/4, 5, and 5 x 3 1/2 in. diam.
(14.5, 12.5, 12.5 x 9 cm).
Firing temperature: 1760°F (960°C).

BURNISHING

With fine clays, a burnished surface will give a more brilliant, perfect surface, while a clay with grog in it will turn out pitted because some of the grog will come off during the process. Burnishing is very effective on pieces with engobe and on thrown pieces, since it emphasizes their color.

Rubbing a rib over the piece while it is on the wheel produces a more intense burnishing. After firing at a low temperature, the shine grows less intense, but it can be made more intense by waxing the piece and rubbing it with a cloth or brush once the wax has dried.

1. For this process you can use the various tools commonly used in ceramics, but they must be able to create a very polished surface. You can also use scissors, pebbles, the handles of other tools, plastic objects, and other things.

2. Throw a vase and decorate it with engobes. When it is leather-hard, burnish it with the convex side of a spoon, using circular movements.

3. After burnishing the whole piece, continue polishing it with one hand inside a plastic bag, which will make the natural shine of the burnishing more brilliant.

Vase, 1998.
5³/₄ x 6³/₄ in.
(14.5 x 16 cm).
Firing temperature:
1760°F (960°C).

Vase, 1998.
4¹/₂ x 5¹/₂ in.
(11.5 x 14 cm).
Firing temperature:
1760°F (960°C).

5. After polishing, you can also burnish thrown pieces with the flat part of a rib. The piece will be further burnished by using the tool to rub the surface of the piece at a tangent and by rotating it at speed.

6. The burnished vase; the vase after bisque-firing.

ENCRUSTING

*E*ncrusting is the process by which colored clay is embedded in a clay of a different color. In order for the process to succeed, both clays must shrink at the same rate to keep the encrustations from coming out or the clay from cracking.

For this method, motifs are cut out of a slab of clay of a certain thickness and placed on top of a different slab. When the rolling pin rolls over them, the motifs that have been cut out are encrusted, slightly deformed, in the clay of the base. This new slab can be modeled to obtain a specific shape.

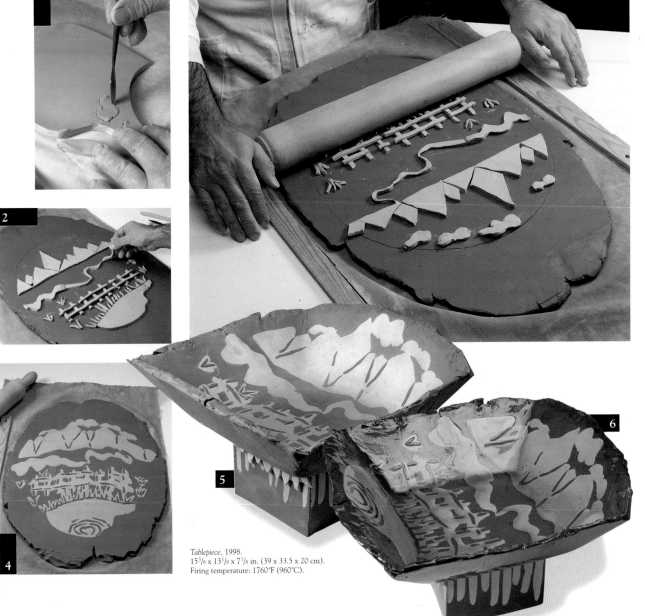

Tablepiece, 1998.
15³/₈ x 13¹/₈ x 7⁷/₈ in. (39 x 33.5 x 20 cm).
Firing temperature: 1760°F (960°C).

1. Prepare a slab of porcelain ³/₈ inch (8 mm) thick and use a metal modeling tool to cut out the motifs that you will then encrust in the red clay.

2. Arrange the porcelain motifs that you have cut out on the slab of red clay, to create the projected drawing.

3. Place a ³/₈-inch (8 mm) slat on either side of the slab of red clay and roll the rolling pin over the motifs, to encrust them in the red clay.

4. The incrustation will look something like this. Notice the slight distortion of the drawing due to the pressure of the rolling pin.

5. For the base I prepared another slab of red clay and encrusted small rolls of porcelain clay in it, using the same process. Then I cut it into four parts to make a square-based prism. To obtain the shape of the center, I used a pyramid-shaped rubber tray covered in a cloth to prevent the clay from sticking to it. I left the piece inside it until it was leather-hard, and then I joined it to the base with slip.

6. After bisque-firing the piece was covered in brilliant, transparent brown glaze.

MISHIMA

A variation of encrusting is a process called mishima, in which grooves are carved in the piece when it is leather-hard, and then later filled with the same type of clay, but in a different color. The grooved parts can be dug out with trimming tools, metal modeling tools, or even a potter's needle. Note that these pieces need to be dried very slowly.

To stop cracks from forming in either the engobe or the piece itself, the drawing can be moistened before it is filled with clay. The clay that is added should be soft, so that it can be encrusted. The drawing should also be filled to above the surface of the base, since it will shrink more than the piece because it has a different degree of dampness. Later the excess can be scraped away with a metal rib and it can be smoothed down.

To create identical decorations, you can make a stamp with which to imprint a motif. The stamp can then be filled according to the method explained here.

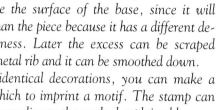

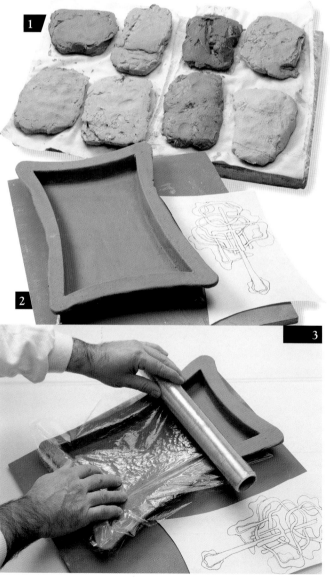

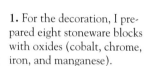

1. For the decoration, I prepared eight stoneware blocks with oxides (cobalt, chrome, iron, and manganese).

2. Next, I modeled the piece using the system of slabs and scoring. This is how the tray looks with the drawing cut to the shape of the base.

3. Place a sheet of plastic over the tray and place the drawing on it, in order to trace it onto the clay.

4. Transfer the drawing using a hard pencil. Use a hand rest to avoid deforming the piece during tracing.

5. Go over the lines of the drawing with a potter's needle; with a metal modeling tool reduce the surface where the colored clay will be inserted. Continue using the hand rest.

6. Detail of the carved motif after using a paintbrush to remove the shavings produced when the clay is carved out.

7. Dampen the carved motif and fill it with colored clay, using a metal modeling tool.

8. You can also use a narrow palette knife to remove the excess clay and join the design to the surface.

9–10. When the piece has dried the inside can be rubbed with fine sandpaper, and the dust removed with a brush.

11. The tray after bisque-firing at 1832°F (1000°C).

12. The tray after applying a matte, transparent glaze.

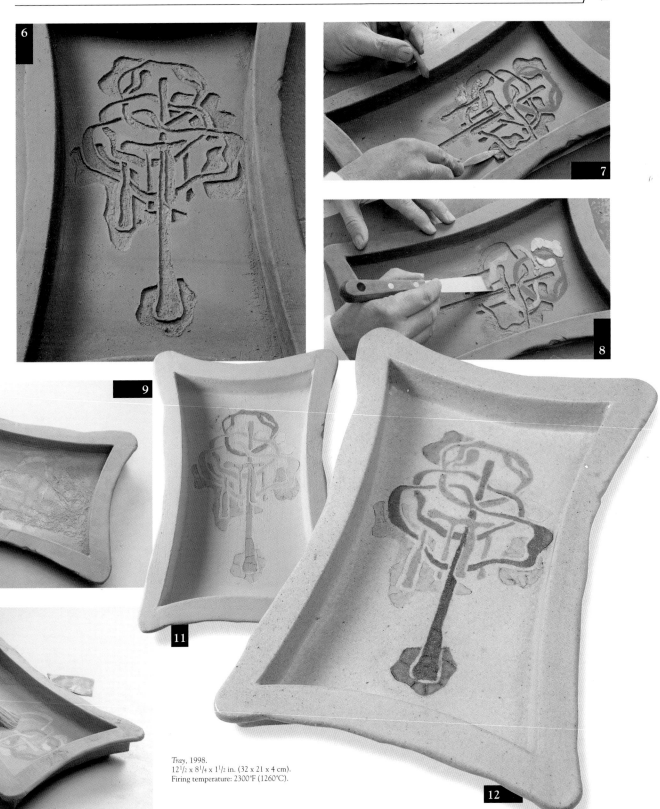

Tray, 1998.
12^1/$_2$ x 8^1/$_4$ x 1^1/$_2$ in. (32 x 21 x 4 cm).
Firing temperature: 2300°F (1260°C).

DECORATING DRY PIECES
OXIDES

*D*ry pieces can also be decorated using metal oxides and with pigments dissolved in water. Nevertheless, remember that the clay in these pieces is not as porous as that in bisque-fired pieces, so the application of the oxides must be done with more care. Also be careful that the load of the paintbrush does not drip onto the surface of the piece, which can create a stain.

It is important that these pieces have fine, compact surfaces, since any scratch or porosity will make the pigment run. To remedy this would require scraping the area again, which would leave it even more porous.

When you have finished decorating these pieces, they can be put in the kiln. If you have used high-temperature clay, the glaze will be fixed after firing. With low-temperature clays you should apply a transparent glaze, which will cover the design and bring out the color of the oxides.

1. Model a slab of stoneware with fine grog, leaving three of the sides as they are when the rolling pin stretches them and cutting the fourth one, which is the one the piece will stand on. Shape it and let it dry. Draw a suitable design and prepare three mortars with oxides (iron, manganese, and chrome) dissolved in water.

2. Since the drawing cannot be transferred to the clay using tracing paper, draw it directly onto the slab of clay with a pencil. To keep the clay from breaking when you lean on it, place the clay on foam for padding. Remember that dry clay is very fragile.

3. Using a fine paintbrush, start to decorate the trees with manganese oxide.

4. Next add the iron oxide and the chrome.

5. To obtain greater chromatic variety, some natural pigments have been applied. This is how the piece looks after bisque-firing at 1832°F (1000°C).

6. In order to show the difference between bisque-firing at low and high temperatures, I fired the piece again at 2300°F (1260°C). The bisque-fired piece could have been covered with a transparent glaze.

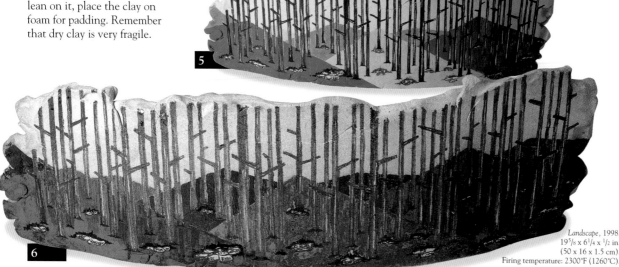

Landscape, 1998.
19⁵/₈ x 6¹/₄ x ¹/₂ in.
(50 x 16 x 1.5 cm).
Firing temperature: 2300°F (1260°C).

SGRAFFITO ON OXIDES

*T*his process is similar to the previous one, but in this case the whole piece is covered with an oxide or with a ceramic pigment. Then the design is drawn freehand with a potter's needle; it is not possible to use either tracing or templates, which would rub away the oxides or pigments.

While the piece is being decorated, do not touch it with your hands or the oxide might rub off or become covered in fingerprints, which would show after firing.

Depending on whether the piece is modeled with high- or low-temperature clays, it should be given one or two firings. Although I used stoneware clay in the exercise below, I fired the piece twice because I wanted to apply a glaze to it.

1. For this exercise throw a cup in two pieces, join them together, and let them dry. You will also need a banding wheel, a potter's needle, and iron oxide dissolved in water.

2. Center the cup on the banding wheel, using the concentric circles in the top of the wheel as a reference. Next, apply the iron oxide.

3. After covering the entire surface with iron oxide, use the potter's needle to decorate it freehand. It is important not to touch the iron oxide with your hands or some of it will be rubbed away and you will have to apply it again.

4. The cup after decorating.

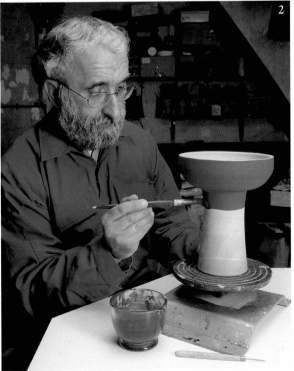

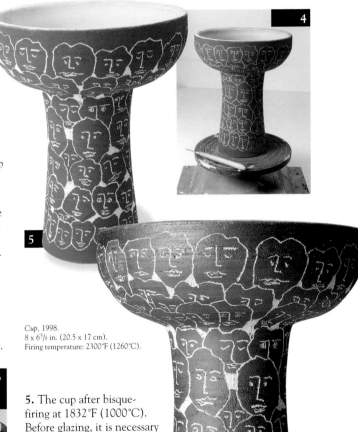

Cup, 1998.
8 x 6⅝ in. (20.5 x 17 cm).
Firing temperature: 2300°F (1260°C).

5. The cup after bisque-firing at 1832°F (1000°C). Before glazing, it is necessary to handle it carefully, as the oxide can still stain.

6. The inside of the piece has been glazed, while the outside has been left unglazed. The color of the iron oxide has darkened with the temperature, and it has also been fixed.

WAX RESISTS

Wax can be used as a resist on unfired pieces to draw motifs that you want to keep free of glaze, in this case the oxide that is applied on top of it.

This particular method utilizes liquid wax, available from ceramics suppliers. It can also be made by mixing 50 percent wax and paraffin and warming both substances in a bain marie on a hot plate. The mixture must be applied warm, or it will harden.

After creating the pattern, the wax is left to cool, and then the oxide or pigments with water are applied to the piece. Since the piece has not been fired, it will absorb them, while the parts covered with wax will repel them. The piece can then be bisque-fired at low or high temperature and the process can be completed as explained earlier.

1. The plate, manganese dioxide, wax, and brushes.

2. Remove any dust from the plate, then use the paintbrush to paint the motif on the inside of the plate with the liquid wax.

3. Decorate the sides of the plate using the same process. Here I have decorated it with a kind of graphic pattern.

4. Leave the wax to dry before applying the manganese dioxide. To make it easier to work, place the plate on a banding wheel and rotate it with the other hand while working on the inside of the plate.

5. Because the wax was not thick enough in some places, when the manganese dioxide was applied it smudged the motif.

6. The plate after bisque-firing at high temperature.

Plate, 1998.
10⅝ in. diam. (27 cm).
Firing temperature:
2300°F
(1260°C).

OTHER RESISTS

*I*n addition to wax, other resists can be used on unfired pieces, including as paper, latex, and various
objects. In these exercises I am going to decorate tiles
with each of these types of resist, and I want to
emphasize the design of the corner tiles, since only
hand-decorated tiles have designs that form an angle.

Strips of paper, latex, or objects, held in place by
small fragments of bisque-fired clay, cover the spaces
that will keep the color of fired clay,
while the other areas will be bathed in
pigments or oxides, in this case applied
with a vaporizer. To produce a whole
series of tiles, you could use a spray gun
designed for ceramics. After firing, a
transparent glaze is applied to the tiles.

1. I place five leaves on four
tiles each measuring 6 x 6 x
³/₈ inches (15 x 15 x 1 cm),
which I hold down with
small pieces of bisque-fired
clay, and vaporize iron oxide
over them.

2. The appearance of the
tiles before bisque-firing. I
have added another tile.

3. The same tiles covered
with transparent glaze.

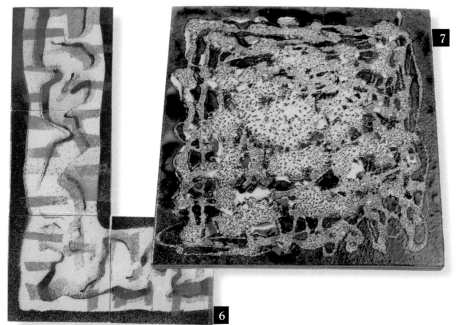

4. Here I am decorating using paper resists. Cut out
strips of paper and hold
them down using pieces of
bisque-fired clay, then vaporize iron oxide over them.

5. With a different color
each time (using oxides and
pigments), continue to cover
the tiles with more strips of
paper, then bisque-fire them.

6. The glazed tiles after
firing.

7. Another example of decorating using resists, this time
with latex. After bisque-firing, a transparent glaze is applied and they are fired
again.

SGRAFFITO ON ENGOBE

Y̶ou can decorate a piece covered with engobe by scraping away the surface of the engobe until you get to the color of the clay. This method of decorating can be used for lines, volumes, or a combination of the two.

The following exercise uses volumes to build pattern on tiles, which can then be used to cover a wall, a tabletop, or other surface. As with the previous exercises, notice the corner tile.

The tool required to scrape away the engobe is a metal modeling tool or a saw blade that has been cut at an angle and then sharpened. When scraping, be careful not to scratch the surface of the tile itself.

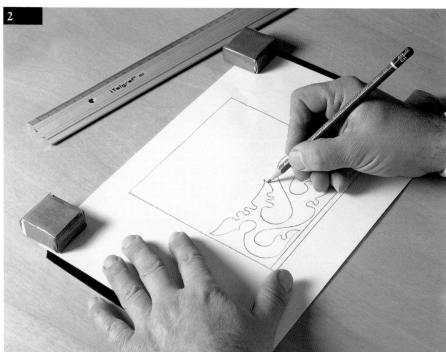

1. For this exercise you can use the same type of tiles as in the last exercise. Prepare a motif of a frieze and a corner piece.

2. You will also need a mirror-image of the motif, so place a sheet of carbon paper facing upward, with a sheet of white paper on top of it, and the drawing on top of that. Trace over the motif. You could also use transparent paper, and use both sides of the template.

3–4. The reproduced drawing along with the original, and the corner motif placed on a tile, before tracing around it.

5. Tracing around the previous image.

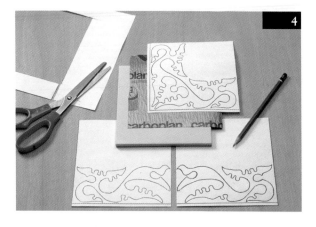

6. Use the potter's needle to go over the drawing, removing the engobe from the tile.

7. Another way of transferring the design onto the tile is to cut out templates, if the design allows it.

8. Use a brush to remove the dust from the tiles.

9. Next, with a saw blade or other metal implement, scratch away the surface of the engobe and again remove the dust with the brush.

10. The tiles, with sgraffito, before bisque-firing.

11. After firing, cover the tiles with a transparent glaze.

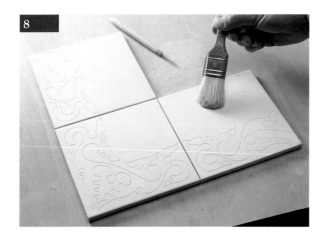

DECORATING BISQUE-FIRED PIECES
UNDERGLAZING USING CERAMIC PENCILS

*T*his method of decoration is done with oxides, pigments, and ceramic pencils on a bisque-fired piece, generally of white clay, which after decorating is covered with a transparent glaze and fired again. During the decoration process, it is important to keep both the piece and your hands clean.

Ceramic pencils are used on a piece's surface, which is smooth and polished. The design can be traced or drawn freehand. The pencils, used like colored pencils, allow colors to be superimposed. Decorating with them requires practice and a great deal of precision, since they cannot be erased.

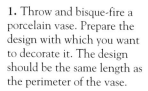

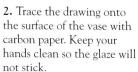

1. Throw and bisque-fire a porcelain vase. Prepare the design with which you want to decorate it. The design should be the same length as the perimeter of the vase.

2. Trace the drawing onto the surface of the vase with carbon paper. Keep your hands clean so the glaze will not stick.

3–4. The decorating process using ceramic pencils.

5. Detail of the finished vase.

6. Cover the inside of the vase with a brilliant, opaque white glaze, and the outside with a transparent glaze.

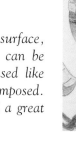

Vase, 1998. 10 x 6⅝ in. (25.5 x 17 cm). Firing temperature: 1760°F (960°C).

UNDERGLAZING USING PIGMENTS

Another method of underglaze decoration is to use oxides and pigments. These materials are mixed with 10 to 15 percent of the same transparent glaze, so that the colors adhere better to the bisque-fired piece. The decoration is drawn with fine lines directly onto the piece with a hard pencil, or it can be traced onto the piece. The carbon in the carbon paper or the graphite pencil will burn off during firing.

For this decoration, it is a good idea to use white clays, which will highlight the color. Before applying the colors, the piece should be clean and dust-free. It can be moistened so that the bisque does not absorb the color from the paintbrush too fast. The color is applied using fine paintbrushes, without loading them with too much color. Your brushstrokes should be firm and quick. It is also possible to decorate with sgraffito using a potter's needle, when the paint is either damp or dry.

The covering should be applied in a fine layer using a spray gun and compressor, so that the drawing shows through underneath. If the glaze is applied too thickly, the result will look milky. Raw glazes can attack some colors, and either smudge or erase them.

3. The decorating process. Before applying the pigments it is important to remove the dust from the piece.

4. Once you have painted the motif, center the piece on a banding wheel to paint the border, applying green coloring to the bottom of the piece with a paintbrush while turning the banding wheel.

5. The piece with the finished decoration. Use a potter's needle to sgraffito some parts of the motif. Then wash the inside of the piece with brilliant, opaque white glaze, and the outside with a transparent glaze.

6. The vase after glaze firing.

1. Throw a cylindrical vase in porcelain and after bisque-firing draw the design on a strip of paper whose length is the same as the perimeter of the cylinder. Wrap a sheet of carbon paper around the vase and place the drawing on top of it, holding it in place with adhesive tape. Go over the drawing with a hard pencil.

2. The vase with the traced design, the paintbrushes that might be used, and the colors required.

Vase, 1998.
9 x 6 in. (23 x 15 cm).
Firing temperature: 1760°F (960°C).

CUERDA SECA

*T*his method is used to separate glazes of different colors and to prevent them from mixing. It is prepared using manganese dioxide, adding about 15 to 20 percent of transparent glaze; mix the materials in a mortar. The result is a black dust that is then mixed with turpentine diluted with turpentine oil; this enables the paintbrush to move easily over the bisque surface. Since the mixture evaporates rapidly, just prepare it as you need it, making only a little at a time. The leftover can be kept in a closed container, covered with a light layer of turpentine. Other oxides and pigments can also be used.

After firing, check whether the cuerda seca stains, by passing a finger over it. If it does, you have to apply the cuerda seca again, increasing the percentage of flux.

Before glazing check that the pattern you have made using this process is completely dry, so that the glaze will not be discolored by absorbing part of the damp cuerda seca.

1. For this decoration use four red clay tiles, each measuring 7 7/8 x 7 7/8 x 3/8 inches (20 x 20 x 1 cm).

2. Place the four tiles together, with the carbon paper and the design on top of them, held down by four weights. You should also use a hand rest so that you do not lean on the drawing.

3. Detail of the design traced onto the tiles.

4. Next, prepare the cuerda seca. For this you will need a piece of glass for mixing on, a mortar, a palette knife, manganese dioxide, and flux.

5. On a separate sheet of paper, draw the border frieze, trace it onto the tiles using the same process as before, and apply the cuerda seca.

6. As you use up the cuerda seca, make more by adding the dry mixture and turpentine. Stir it with a palette knife.

7. After painting on the cuerda seca, let it dry completely before painting on the glaze.

8. Glazes used to decorate the insides of the cuerda seca and samples of the colors that result from firing each of them.

9. Detail of the glazing process. Note the use of a hand rest to avoid brushing against the surface of the cuerda seca.

10. When you have finished decorating the figure, move the tiles slightly apart while you glaze the background and the borders, otherwise the glaze will cover the join and would break when you separated them.

11. Detail of the application of glaze to the background. Large areas can be glazed with a palette knife, which allows the glaze to be applied more quickly and uniformly.

12–13. The cuerda seca before and after firing.

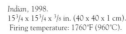

Indian, 1998.
15³/₄ x 15³/₄ x ³/₈ in. (40 x 40 x 1 cm).
Firing temperature: 1760°F (960°C).

DECORATING GLAZED PIECES
RESISTS

*T*hese are used to cover areas of the pieces so that they do not get covered by glaze. Latex, wax, and paper are the most common materials used for ceramic resists; they can also be used on unfired and bisque-fired pieces as well as glazed ones.

The positioning of the resists must be adapted to the shape of the piece. Wax and latex can be applied to any piece, but paper resists are better on flat surfaces. Wax and latex can be left on the piece since they will burn away during firing; paper resists must be removed once the glaze is dry.

Oxides and pigments can be applied dry, by dusting them on, or wet with an airbrush, paintbrush, toothbrush, or the like.

Latex

1. Throw a vase of stoneware with fine-grained grog, bisque-fire it, and cover it with a white feldspar glaze. Apply rivulets of latex to the glazed surface and wait for it to dry.

2. Place the vase on a banding wheel and vaporize blue coloring over it, diluted in water.

3. The vase before being placed in the kiln.

4–5. The vase after firing, during which the latex has burned away, revealing the glaze beneath. Detail of the patterning.

Vase, 1998.
18³/₄ x 8⁵/₈ in. (47.5 x 22 cm).
Firing temperature: 2300°F (1260°C).

Wax

6. Wash a thrown stoneware bowl with glaze, first on the inside and then on the outside.

7. Apply liquid wax on top of the glaze, using a paintbrush.

8–9. Let the wax dry and glaze the inside and the outside of the bowl again with a darker glaze.

10. During firing the wax resist will disappear. The results of this type of decoration are unpredictable, since when the wax melts, the glaze spreads out, which could alter the design of the piece. This does not happen if the piece is flat. In this case the glaze has maintained its vertical lines, while the horizontal lines have become blurred.

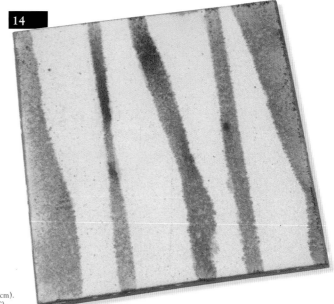

Bowl, 1998.
$3^1/2$ x $8^5/8$ in. (9 x 22 cm).
Firing temperature: 2300°F (1260°C).

Paper

11. With a wide paintbrush, apply four layers of glaze to a bisque-fired tile, painting in both directions.

12. Cut out four strips of wrapping paper and place them on the tile, then go over the spaces between them with another glaze.

13. Dust some cobalt carbonate on top of this to increase the intensity. When the glaze is dry, remove the paper resists.

14. The tile after it has been fired.

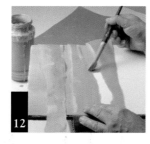

Tile, 1998.
$12^1/4$ x $12^1/4$ x $1/2$ in. (31 x 31 x 1.2 cm).
Firing temperature: 2300°F (1260°C).

OVERGLAZING

*T*his type of decoration is applied over an enamel (generally opaque white) that covers a bisque-fired piece. The glaze covering, to which will be added an adhesive (gum arabic) to aid its application and subsequent manipulation, can be applied by pouring, dipping, or spraying. The first two methods tend to give better results because the glaze will be smooth and polished; applied with an airbrush the glaze will form tiny droplets, which will be visible when you add colors with a paintbrush.

The design can be made directly on the glaze or can be traced with a stencil. The colors used are oxides and pigments, dry mixed with 10 percent transparent glaze, which will make it melt and meld better with the glaze covering. The components are diluted with water so that the paintbrush will flow easily over the surface. After decorating the surface, a light layer of transparent glaze is added.

The way of applying the color is similar to water-color painting: since the raw glaze absorbs the color quickly, the brushstrokes must be firm and quick. Mistakes are difficult to correct because it is not possible to erase the color completely; the covering will have absorbed it.

1. Turn a plate to decorate using this technique, and prepare everything to wash the interior with glaze.

2. Pour glaze over the interior of the plate until it is completely covered, returning the excess glaze to the receptacle. Repeat the operation with the reverse side.

3. Make a drawing on a circle of paper the same size as the interior of the plate, and another to fit the border. Place the drawings on a sheet of cardboard and punch holes through it with a pin.

4. The perforated drawing.

5. Place the drawing inside the plate. Pour ochre pigment onto a cloth to make an applicator with which to stencil the motif.

6. Hold the paper with one hand and stencil with the other.

7. The pigment passes through the holes and marks the design on the piece.

8. Paint the pigments onto the surface of the plate with a fine paintbrush.

9. The plate during the decorating process, with the central motif already finished.

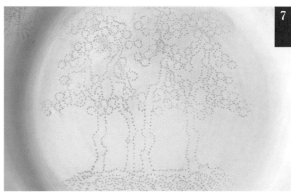

10. After painting the three motifs on the border, center the plate on a banding wheel and paint the borders of the inner and outer circles with a paintbrush. The ochre pigment will disappear during firing.

11. Finally, before firing, apply a fine layer of transparent glaze to cover the design. This is how the finished plate looks after firing.

Plate, 1998.
10⁵/₈ in. diam. (27 cm).
Firing temperature: 1760°F (960°C).

OIL-BASED OVERGLAZING

*T*his variation of the previous process is used to decorate pieces covered in glaze that have already been fired. Before beginning the decoration, the piece must be clean, dry, and dust-free. The design can be transferred onto the piece using carbon paper.

The colors are mixed with 20 to 30 percent of an oil solvent, which is available from ceramics suppliers. You can also use turpentine essence, which can be diluted with a little turpentine if it is very thick. Mix the colors with the oil on a sheet of glass, using a palette knife, until they reach a uniform, fluid consistency.

Besides a paintbrush, a pen and nib are also very useful for drawing the design. In this case the color should be dissolved a little more and the nib cleaned, since the color will dry very quickly, preventing it from marking the image.

It is easy to correct mistakes with this kind of decoration because the glaze does not absorb the color; simply remove it by scraping it off the surface and paint over it again.

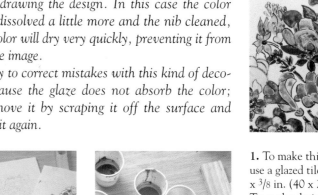

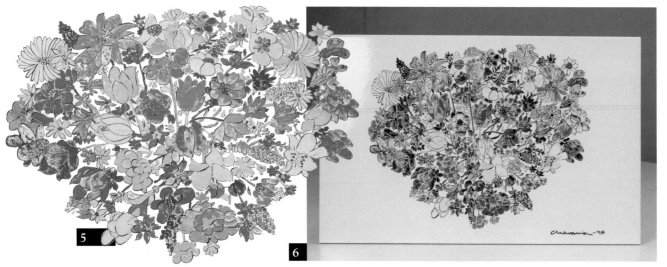

1. To make this decoration, use a glazed tile 15 3/4 x 9 7/8 x 3/8 in. (40 x 25 x 0.8 cm). Trace the design onto it. Place a sheet of carbon paper on the clean, dust-free tile and lay the drawing on top of it, taping it in place at each side. Use a hand rest so as not to press on the tracing paper, and go over the design using a hard pencil.

2. The drawing traced onto the tile.

3. Prepare the black pigment with essence of turpentine, trying to ensure that it remains fluid. Go over the design again with a pen and nib.

4. Repeat the same process with the other pigments and begin to color in the design. If you make a mistake, allow the area you have painted to dry and then scrape the paint off.

5. The freshly painted drawing, before putting the tile in the kiln.

6. The tile after firing.

Flowers, 1998.
15 3/4 x 9 7/8 x 3/8 in. (40 x 25 x 0.8 cm).
Firing temperature: 1760°F (960°C).

SUPERIMPOSING GLAZES

*I*n this process, various glazes are superimposed so that they react in different ways and mix together. Gum arabic is added to these glazes so that they stick to one another better. The results are difficult to predict, even if you've tested them beforehand to see how each glaze reacts. The outcome depends on such factors as the thickness of the glaze, how it was applied, and the shape of the piece.

The best results are obtained with concave pieces, in which the glaze tends to accumulate in the bottom, producing very interesting results. Good results can also be obtained from flat pieces if the glaze is thick enough. With vertical-sided pieces, as a precaution it is better to raise them a little or to place them on a support covered in aluminum oxide, which will make it easier to lift the piece off in case the glaze runs.

This method can also be used on pieces that have already been glazed and fired, if you wish to alter the appearance of the surface. It can also be used on pieces that have not been glazed properly, or which have defects, if they are correctable.

Before applying the new glaze, the pieces are warmed in the kiln so that the glaze sticks to the surface. When the glaze comes into contact with a warm object, the water evaporates, leaving the glaze as a dust. You must handle these pieces with extreme care; it is a good idea to glaze them on the same stand on which they are going to be fired, to avoid touching them with your hands.

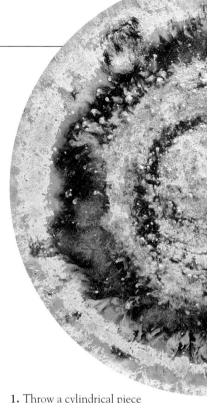

1. Throw a cylindrical piece using stoneware with fine-grained grog. Glaze the inside with a blue color, rotating it with your hands.

2. Apply a fine layer of glaze to the outside of the piece, and then pour a second, lighter glaze over the first one.

3. Stand the piece upright and use a paintbrush to let glaze flow down the inside, leaving some areas free of glaze. Fire the piece.

4–5. The second application of glaze in a thicker layer covers the color of the first glaze, creating areas of transparency on the outside, while accumulating along the lip, the internal grooves, and particularly in the base.

6. A retouched piece that had been fired without enough glaze.

Cylinder, 1998.
8⅝ x 6⅝ in. (22 x 17 cm).
Firing temperature: 2300°F (1260°C).

Bowl, 1998.
4 x 15 in. (10 x 38 cm).
Firing temperature: 2300°F (1260°C).

SGRAFFITO

*I*n the same way that sgraffito can be used with engobe, it is also possible to apply it to glazes, although in this case the fragility of raw glaze makes it more difficult. It is more practical to apply sgraffito to flat pieces than to vertical ones, unless you use a glaze that has been thoroughly tested and that does not run. In both cases, gum arabic is applied so that the glaze has less of a tendency to break during the process.

The most suitable tool is a potter's needle, as well as a metal modeling tool or a fine teaspoon for removing large amounts of glaze. A fine paintbrush with strong, short bristles is useful for cleaning the glaze from the lines and areas of sgraffito. After completing the sgraffito, the piece is covered with a fine layer of transparent glaze. The piece should be fired at a temperature that will not cause the glaze to run and thus partially cover the sgraffito.

1. For this exercise you need four 7⅞ x 7⅞ x ⅜ in. (20 x 20 x 1 cm) bisque-fired tiles. Apply the glaze by pouring.

2–3. First apply a layer of glaze by moving the tile with your hand so that it is totally covered, and then repeat the process so that the glaze is sufficiently thick.

4. Let the tiles dry on two slats. When they are dry to the touch, use a clean, stiff brush to apply glaze to the backs and sides.

5. The four tiles and the design.

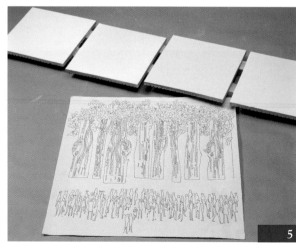

6. Place the four tiles in the form of a square, and cover it with a sheet of fine plastic, taped to the table so that it does not move. Place the drawing on top of this. It should be the same size as the tiles. Use a hand rest so that you do not smudge the glaze as you go over the drawing.

7. The tiles with the drawing engraved in the glaze.

8. Begin the sgraffito by removing glaze from inside the drawn areas with a potter's needle, again using the hand rest. Use a bulb to remove the extra glaze.

9. With a fine, short, stiff paintbrush, clean inside the areas of sgraffito.

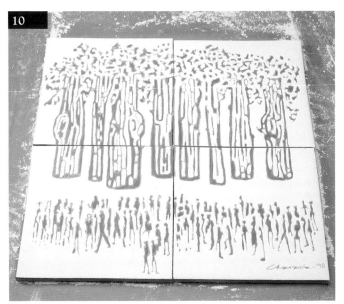

10. The finished sgraffito.

11. Finally, apply a fine layer of transparent glaze with a spray gun and fire the piece.

12. The finished mural.

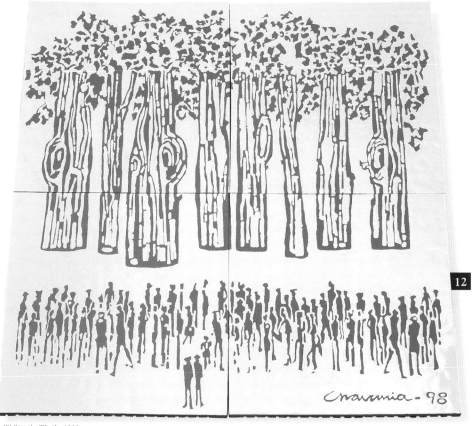

A Walk in the Woods, 1998.
15 1/4 x 15 3/4 x 3/8 in. (40 x 40 x 1 cm).
Firing temperature: 1760°F (960°C).

GLOSSARY

Alumina. Aluminum oxide (Al_2O_3). Substance placed on the trays that support glazed pieces to prevent the glaze from sticking if it runs.

Bain marie. Apparatus for heating something gently: the contents requiring heating are placed in a receptacle that in turn is placed inside another receptacle containing water.

Canvas. A strong cloth made from cotton or hemp.

Costume jewelry. Decorative adornments that are not made from precious materials.

Concave. A curved line or surface that, in relation to the eye, is most hollow in the center.

Concentric. Figures and objects with the same center.

Convex. A curved line or surface that, in relation to the eye, is most prominent in the center.

Covering. A glaze applied to a piece, on top of which the decoration is made.

Cuerda seca. A method of decorating using lines of oxide to separate different colors.

Cutters. Tools with sharp edges, used for cutting out small pieces of clay, by pressing down on a thin slab of clay.

Dilute. To dissolve the parts of some substances using a liquid.

Dodecagon. A regular polygon with twelve sides.

Facets. Faces that are created by cutting or paddling a ceramic piece.

Flap. A portion of excess material that sticks out over an edge.

Fluting. Longitudinal grooves or furrows.

Frieze. A repeated decorative design, especially along a wall.

Fretting. Decoration consisting of perforations.

Furrow. A long, straight groove.

Grog. Bisque-fired clay ground to different degrees of coarseness; it is an inelastic material that aids the drying of clay and increases the strength of pieces during firing.

Hand rest. A wooden slat placed on other blocks of wood to support the hands, so as not to touch the surface of a piece or drawing.

Hemispherical. Something that has the shape of half a sphere.

Hessian. A very coarse, burlap-type material on which ceramic clay can be placed without sticking.

Hexagon. A regular polygon with six sides.

Hollow out. To make a cavity deeper.

Hypotenuse. The side opposite the right angle in a right-angle triangle.

Imprint. A mark or impression left by an object that is pressed onto another; a print or stamp.

Incense burner. A bowl for burning perfume.

Incision. A cut made in a surface using a sharp tool.

Jasperized. Veined or sprinkled with markings like jasper.

Join. The line where two surfaces intersect.

Leather-hard. The state of red clay or other ceramic pastes when they are partially hardened but are still a little damp.

Oxide. The combination of an element with oxygen. Many of the materials used in ceramics are oxides or combinations of oxides.

Perimeter. The outer edge of a surface or shape.

Perpendicular bisector. The line perpendicular to another that divides it into two equal parts.

Pigment. A coloring material.

Polygon. Part of a plane, delimited by straight lines.

Relief. A form or figure that sticks out from a surface.

Resist. Wax, latex, paper, or other substances applied to a surface to cover it while the surrounding area is treated with another color.

Retouch. A correction made to a work to remove errors and fix small imperfections.

Sandpaper. A sheet of strong paper with ground glass stuck to one of its sides.

Set square. A template made of wood, plastic, or any other material, in the form of a right-angled, scalene triangle.

Settle. When materials held in suspension in a liquid form a sediment.

Slat. A thin, narrow length of wood.

Stencil. A drawing made by placing over it another drawing with holes in it, onto which pigment is applied.

Support. A piece in the form of a plate, with a foot in the center against which another glazed piece is supported. When covered in alumina, the piece on top will not stick if its glaze runs.

Terra-cotta. Porous, reddish ceramic clay containing grog, cooked at low temperature, 1652–1832°F (900–1000°C). It literally means "cooked earth."

Texture. Irregularities in the surface of a piece.

Turpentine. A solvent.

Turpentine oil. The volatile oil of turpentine.

Vein. Band or stripe of a substance that stands out against the substance in which it is interspersed because of its consistency, color, or other characteristic.